।। न हि ज्ञानेन सदृशं पवित्रमिह विद्यते ।।

MW00445742

Pūrṇa Vidyā

(Vedic Heritage Teaching Programme)

Pūjā & Prayers

*"One's wisdom and appreciation of beauty manifests through various forms of one's culture.
And the study of one's cultural heritage leads one to the appreciation of beauty and wisdom in life."*
Swami Dayananda

Swamini Pramananda and Sri Dhira Chaitanya

Editor: Irene Schleicher

FIRST EDITION 2011

Published by
Swamini Pramananda and Sri Dhira Chaitanya

Books Available at:

In India

Purna Vidya Trust, Headquarters
"Mamatha", # 8A, Basement,
North Gopalapuram IInd Street,
Chennai – 600086 (India)
Phone: 044-2835 2593
E. Mail: **purnavidyachennai@gmail.com**

In U.S.A
E.Mail: **purnavidyausa@gmail.com**
Phone: 1-718-501-4785

In U.K
E.Mail: **purnavidya.uk@gmail.com**
Phone: +44-19522-73543

For more information on other Books/Cds/ Vcds of Purna Vidya visit the website: **http://www.purnavidya.com**

Printed by: Ratna Offset Printers, 40, Peters Road, Royapettah, Chennai - 600 014.

कृष्णाय वासुदेवाय देवकीनन्दनाय च ।
नन्दगोपकुमाराय गोविन्दाय नमो नमः ।।

kṛṣṇāya vāsudevāya devakī nandanāya ca
nandagopakumāraya govindāya namo namaḥ

Salutations to Lord *Kṛṣṇa*, the son of *Vāsudeva*, who delights *Devakī*, who is the son of *Nandagopa* and who is called *Govinda*.

Table of Contents

Message from Swamiji

Water may be available underground, but one can have it only by the effort of tapping. The grace of the Lord is always for everyone, but one has to earn it. The sure way of earning it is by prayer in the form of *pūjā* (worship), recitation and also, mental japa. If you study and practice the material in this '*Pūjā* and Prayers' book, you will have the means of earning *Bhagavān's* grace all your lifetime. Learn to chant and recite properly. One has to pay attention to pronunciation and the mode of chanting. The meanings of the chants and verses also have to be learned carefully. May the Lord's grace be with you to earn his grace.

Swami Dayananda Saraswati

Authors' Note

The '*Pūjā* and Prayers' book is a supplement to your study of the Vedic Heritage. The three audio-tapes (one Cd) are instructional aids to help you in correct pronunciation of the Sanskrit *mantras*. The prayers are in the form of *ślokas* and *stotras* and are to be studied over a period of ten years, as described in the syllabus (Part1 to Part 10).

As you learn to perform the *pūjā*, you will discover the beauty of this physicalised expression of your devotion and appreciate the richness that lies in the forms of our religious culture. Identifying with these simple and profound forms of worship, you will discover the devotee within, the fundamental relationship of the created with the creator. It is this discovery that is the greatest blessing of a human life taking the person to the heights of spiritual wisdom.

Swamini Pramananda Saraswati and Sri Dhira Chaitanya

Key to Transliteration

Key to Transliteration and Pronunciation of Sanskrit Letters

Since Sanskrit is a highly phonetic language, accuracy in articulation of . letters is important.For those unfamiliar with *Devanāgarī* script, the international transliteration is a guide to proper pronunciation of Sanskrit letters.

अ	*a* (but)
आ	*ā* (mom)
इ	*i* (it)
ई	*ī* (beet)
उ	*u* (put)
ऊ	*ū* (pool) ð
ऋ	*ṛ* (rhythm)
ए	*e* (play)
ऐ	*ai* (high)
ओ	*o* (toe)
औ	*au* (loud)
क	*k* (skate) 1
ख	*kh* (blockhead)*1
ग	*g* (gate) 1
घ	*gh* (loghut)*1
ङ्	*ṅ* (sing) 1
च	*c* (chunk) 2
छ	*ch* (catch him)*2
ज	*j* (john) 2
झ	*jh* (hedgehog)*2
ञ	*ñ* (bunch) 2
ट	*ṭ* (start)*3 õ
ठ	*ṭh* (anthill)*3 ö
ड	*ḍ* (dart)*3 ÷
ण	*ṇ* (under)*3
ढ	*ḍh* (godhead)*3
फ	*ph* (loophole)*5
ब	*b* (bin) 5
भ	*bh* (abhor)*5
म	*m* (much) 5
य	*y* (young)
र	*r* (drama) ú
त	*t* (path)*4
थ	*th* (thunder)*4
द	*d* (that)*4
ध	*dh* (breathe)*4
न	*n* (numb)*4
प	*p* (spin) 5
ल	*l* (luck)
व	*v* (in between wile and vile)
श	*ś* (shove)
ष	*ṣ* (bushel)
स	*s* (so)
ह	*h* (hum)
ṃ	*anusavāra* (nasalise preceding vowel)
ḥ	*visarga* (aspirate preceding vowel)

* No exact English equivalents for these.

1-guttural;2-palatal;3-lingual;4-dental;5-labial

Pūjā

Pūjā

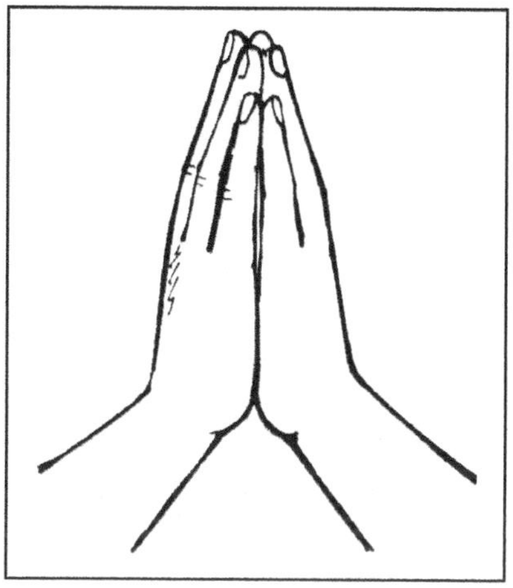

WHAT IS *PŪJĀ*?

Pūjā is one of the most beautiful ways to bring out the devotee within oneself and establish a relationship with *Īśvara*, the Lord. *Pūjā* is called *kāyikaṃ-karma*, an action involving one's limbs. It also includes speech and mental action in the form of chanting and thinking of the Lord.

In a physical form of worship, such as a *pūjā*, there is a greater field of expression of one's devotion than is possible in purely oral or mental forms of worship. The body, mind and speech are all involved in a *pūjā*. The forms, colours, fragrances and sounds of the various items of worship arrest one's mind and aid in evoking devotion in oneself.

A *pūjā* is performed in order to express one's gratitude to *Īśvara* for all one has been given in one's life. The very creation in which one is born is considered to be a gift of the Lord. The body-mind-sense complex is made up of five basic elements: space, air, fire, water and earth which also constitute the creation. Through the sense perceptions backed by the mind one perceives the Lord's vast creation and appreciates his glories.

Traditionally, a form of worship known as *pañcopacara-pūjā*, worship with fivefold offering, is performed. This worship acknowledges the presence of the Lord and makes a simple offering of the five elements through a symbolic offering of *puṣpa*, flowers; *dhūpa*, incense; *dīpa*, light; *naivedya*, food and *gandha*, sandalwood paste. These objects represent the elements space, air, fire, water and earth, respectively.

Pūjā at Home

Pūjā is generally performed by an individual at home. Most homes have an altar where one or more deities are kept. The choice of deity is a personal one. It does not matter which deity is chosen as each one represents *Īśvara* in a different form or aspect. The deity that one chooses is called *Iṣṭa-devatā*, one's desired deity.

Pañcāyatana Pūjā

Traditionally, those who strictly follow the Vedic way of life perform a *pūjā* called the *pañcāyatana-pūjā*. The following verse describes the deities worshipped in this *pūjā*:

आदित्यम् अम्बिकां विष्णुं गणनाथं महेश्वरम्।
पञ्चयज्ञपरो नित्यं गृहस्थः पञ्च पूजयेत्॥

ādityam ambikāṃ viṣṇuṃ gaṇanāthaṃ maheśvaram
pañcayajñaparo nityaṃ gṛhasthaḥ pañca pūjayet

ādityam - the sun deity; *ambikām* - Goddess *Ambikā*; *viṣṇum* - Lord *Viṣṇu*; *gaṇanātham* - Lord *Gaṇeśa*; *maheśvaram* - Lord *Śiva*; *pañca-yajña-paraḥ* - one committed to the five sacrifices; *nityam* - daily; *gṛhasthaḥ* - householder; *pañca* - five; *pūjayet* - may worship

"A householder who is committed to the performance of the *paca-yajas*, five daily sacrifices, may do *pañcāyatana-pūjā* daily to five deities: the sun deity, Goddess *Ambikā*, Lord *Viṣṇu*, Lord *Gaṇeśa* and Lord *Śiva*."

The five deities in this *pūjā* are traditionally invoked in the form of naturally occurring stones. For instance, *sphaṭika*, a crystal which occurs in various places in India, represents *Āditya* (the sun deity); stones with specific markings, obtained from River *Svarṇamukhī* in Andhra Pradesh, represents Goddess *Ambikā*; *śāligrāma*, obtained from River *Gaṇḍakī* in Nepal, represents Lord *Viṣṇu*; a red stone called *śoṇabadra* from River *Śoṇa* represents Lord *Gaṇeśa*; and *bāṇaliṅga*, obtained from River *Narmadā*, represents Lord *Śiva*.

The idols are placed in a prescribed manner. For *Śiva-pañcāyatana -pūjā*, Lord *Śiva* is placed in the centre, surrounded by the other deities; for *Viṣṇu-pañcāyatana-pūjā Viṣṇu* is is placed in the centre, surrounded by the other deities, and so on.

A *pūjā* is performed to all the deities in either a five-step worship or a sixteen-step worship.

Steps of a *Pūjā*

Whether a *pūjā* is performed at home or in a temple, the essential steps are the same. The basic *pūjā* is called the *pañcopacāra-pūjā*, in which one makes a fivefold offering. A more elaborate *pūjā* is called the *ṣoḍaśopacāra-pūjā*, a sixteen-step *pūjā*, in which one additionally offers clothes, ornaments and other similar items that one enjoys. The most elaborate *pūjā* is called the *catuṣṣaṣṭi-upacāra-pūjā*, a sixty-four step *pūjā*, where the offerings include music, dance, chariots, elephants and other similar items. Whatever one enjoys in life can be offered to the Lord as an expression of gratitude.

With minor variations, the following steps are customarily followed in any *pūjā*. After taking a bath and preparing the altar, one sits in front of the altar in a comfortable posture. One begins the *pūjā* by lighting a lamp, which symbolises knowledge. In order to be prayerful, one invokes an attitude of purity within oneself by doing *ācamana*, which involves chanting the Lord's name three times and sipping water with each chant. This is followed by a prayer to Lord *Gaṇeśa*, who is the remover of all obstacles. Next, one performs *prāṇāyāma*, which helps one gain a relative composure of mind. *Saṅkalpa* is done next to identify the person, *yajamāna*, doing the *pūjā*, and to state the purpose for which the *pūjā* is done. Then one rings the bell. The sound of the bell is considered auspicious and is said to ward off negative influences from the place of worship.

Following these steps, one sanctifies water in the water pot through chants and purifies the various articles of worship by sprinkling the sanctified water on them. These articles include the place where one is seated, the bell and the flowers.

The *yajamāna* then offers prayers to the Lord within himself by reciting a verse in which one's body is likened to a temple and the self within is likened to the deity. As a final preparatory step one offers prayers to one's *guru*.

The main *pūjā* may be brief or elaborate. It begins by invoking the presence of the Lord in a given symbol. This symbol may be a picture or an idol of a given deity, such as *Gaṇeśa* or *Lakṣmī*; or even a lump of turmeric powder; a betelnut; or a *kalaśa*, a brass pot of water. Once the Lord is invoked, the symbol is looked upon as the Lord until the *pūjā* is completed.

The Lord is treated as a revered guest. He is offered a regal seat and his feet are washed. He is then given a bath and offered clothes and various ornaments. Flowers are offered along with salutations. While offering flowers and salutations, the Lord is addressed by various names. They may be sixteen in number, one hundred and eight in number, or one thousand and eight in number. These names reveal the glories of the Lord and his essential nature. *Naivedya* is offered to the Lord in the form of freshly cooked food or fruits. The Lord is then provided with comforts and music and dance is offered unto him.

After the various offerings are completed, one offers *ārati* to the Lord by lighting a camphor and chanting prayers. Following the *ārati* one offers flowers and salutations. One concludes the worship by asking for forgiveness for any inadequacies, omissions and commissions in the performance of the *pūjā*. Once the *pūjā* is completed, the Lord is requested to return to his abode. The offerings that are made to the Lord are distributed as *prasāda* to everyone who participates in the *pūjā*.

Items Needed to Peform *Pūjā*

The following items are needed to perform the sixteen-step *pūjā*:

- An altar with a *vigraha*, idol, of the deity to be worshipped. If an idol is not available, a picture of the deity may be used.
- An oil lamp, oil and a wick. One lights the lamp at the beginning of the *pūjā* and makes sure that it remains lit until the *pūjā* is completed.
- *Akṣatas*, unbroken rice grains to which turmeric powder is added.
- *Pañcapātra*, a vessel with water and spoon for offering water. The water may be poured into another cup during the offering.
- *Candana*, sandalpaste and *kuṅkuma*, vermilion.
- *Dhūpa*, incense sticks.
- *Vastra*, cloth.
- *dīpa*, a small oil lamp.
- *Naivedya*, food offering.
- *Puṣpa*, flowers kept on a plate.
- *Ghaṇṭā*, bell.
- *Karpūra*, camphor with a holder for burning it.
- The altar should be clean and can be decorated as one wishes. Metal vessels and utensils are preferable. If these are not available, paper plates and cups may be used. The utensils for the *pūjā* should be kept apart and not used for other purposes.

  [If some of the offerings listed above such as *vastra*, *puṣpa* and so on, are not available, one may use *akṣatas* instead.]

Brief Explanation of the Steps

After lighting a lamp, one performs the *saṅkalpa*. The *saṅkalpa* identifies the person doing the *pūjā* (*yajamāna*) and the purpose for which the *pūjā* is done. A common purpose in all *pūjās* is '*durita-kṣaya*' - the removal of *duritas*, impurities of the mind. One may pray for other reasons, but an important element in all prayers is to seek a mind free from confusion and wrong thinking.

The initial step is invoking the presence of the Lord in the given symbol. Once invoked, the symbol becomes the Lord and is looked upon as such until the *pūjā* is completed.

The Lord is received with an attitude of devotion and is then offered *ācamana*, *vastra*, cloth and the other items described.

While offering flowers, one addresses the Lord by the various names that reveal the Lord's nature or describe his glories. One may chant sixteen, one hundred and eight, or one thousand and eight names of the Lord.

Naivedya is then offered at the altar. For *naivedya*, one may offer fruits (fresh or dried), nuts, or cooked foods. It is customary that we do not offer the Lord pre-made, store-bought or leftover foods.

Ārati is performed by dimming or switching off the electric lights in the room and offering lighted camphor.

When visiting a temple, one may go around the deity clockwise three times as an act of salutation. Since the Lord also abides within, one may turn around oneself three times, in a clockwise direction, while remaining in the same spot. Both these acts are known as *pradakṣiṇa* .

In performing the *pūjā*, there may have been errors of omission and commission. One asks for forgiveness of the Lord for these.

After the *pūjā*, the Lord is requested with a prayer to return to his original abode. The *prasāda* is then taken from the altar and distributed to all.

PŪJĀ VIDHĀNAM

Preparatory Steps to the Sixteen-step *Pūjā*:

1. Light a lamp.

2. Offer flowers chanting:

   दीपज्योतिः परं ब्रह्म दीपज्योतिर्जनार्दनः।
   दीपो मे हरतु पापं दीपज्योतिर्नमोऽस्तुते॥

   dīpajyotiḥ paraṃ brahma dīpajyotir janārdanaḥ
   dīpo me haratu pāpaṃ dīpajyotir namo stute

   The light of the lamp stands for *Brahman*, the unmanifest truth as well as for Lord *Viṣṇu* (in his manifest form). Let that light of lamp remove my *pāpas* results of omissions and commissions.

3.a. *Ācamanam*

Take a sip of water after chanting each of the following *mantras*:

ॐ अच्युताय नमः।

oṃ acyutāya namaḥ

Salutation unto the Lord who is imperishable.

ॐ अनन्ताय नमः।

oṃ anantāya namaḥ

Salutation unto the Lord who is limitless.

ॐ गोविन्दाय नमः।

oṃ govindāya namaḥ

Salutation unto Lord *Govinda*.

b. *Guru Dhyānam* - Visualisation of one's *Guru*.

गुरुर्ब्रह्मा गुरुर्विष्णुः गुरुर्देवो महेश्वरः ।
गुरुस्साक्षात् परं ब्रह्म तस्मै श्रीगुरवे नमः।

gururbrahmā gururvishnuḥ gururdevo maheśvarah
gurussākṣat paraṃ brahma tasmai śrī gurave namaḥ

The *guru* is *Brahmā*, the *guru* is *Viṣṇu*, the *guru* is *Maheśvarah*. The *guru* is ultimate truth. Unto that *guru* my prostration.

c. *Vighneśvara Dhyānam* - Visualisation of Lord *Gaṇeśa*.

Lightly tap the temples with the knuckles, chanting the following *mantra*:

शुक्लाम्बरधरं विष्णुं शशिवर्णं चतुर्भुजम्।
प्रसन्नवदनं ध्यायेत् सर्वविघ्नोपशान्तये।।

suklāmbaradharaṃ viṣṇuṃ śaśivarṇaṃ caturbhujam
prasannavadanaṃ dhyāyet sarvavighnopaśāntaye

May one meditate upon Lord *Vighneśvara*, who wears the white garment, who is all pervasive, who has a bright complexion (like the full moon), who has four hands (representing all power), who has an ever-smiling face (or an elephant face), for the removal of all obstacles.

d. *Prāṇāyāmaḥ* - Breath Control

While closing the right nostril with the right thumb, inhale through left nostril chanting mentally:

ॐ भूः। ॐ भुवः। ॐ सुवः। ॐ महः। ॐ जनः। ॐ तपः। ॐ सत्यम् ।

oṃ bhūḥ oṃ bhuvaḥ oṃ suvaḥ oṃ mahaḥ oṃ janaḥ oṃ tapaḥ oṃ satyam

Hold the breath inside by closing the right nostril with the right thumb and left nostril with ring finger, while chanting mentally:

ॐ तत्सवितुर्वरेण्यम् भर्गो देवस्य धीमहि ।
धियो यो नः प्रचोदयात्।

oṃ tatsaviturvareṇyam bhargo devasya dhīmahi
dhiyo yo naḥ pracodayāt

Close the left nostril with the ring finger and exhale through the right nostril chanting mentally:

ॐ आपो ज्योतीरसोऽमृतं ब्रह्म भूर्भुवस्सुवरोम्।।

om āpo jyotiraso'mṛtaṃ brahma bhūrbhuvassuvarom

The seven worlds are pervaded by the Lord the creator. *Om* is the basis of everything. That Lord is the one who is the most worshipful. We meditate on that all-knowing Lord. May he set our intellects in the right direction. The Lord is the waters in the rivers and oceans, the light in the luminaries, the tastes in food, the essence of everything, the body of the *Vedas*, the three-fold worlds and *om*.

4. *Saṅkalpaḥ* - Statement of the Purpose of the *Pūjā*.

Clasp your right palm over the left palm holding a flower; place them on your right thigh. Offer the flower at the altar, after chanting:

ममोपात्त-समस्त-दुरितक्षयद्वारा श्रीपरमेश्वर-प्रीत्यर्थं देवपूजां करिष्ये।।

mamopātta-samasta-duritakṣayadvārā
śrīparameśvara-prītyartham devapūjām krisye

I do the *pūjā* to Lord *Deva** to obtain the grace of the Lord through the removal of all afflictions resulting from my omissions and commissions.

* *Deva* may be substituted by any other deity, such as *Mahāgaṇapati, Mahāviṣṇu, Mahāsarasvatī, Mahālakṣmī*.

5. *Āsana pūjā* - Worship of the Earth to Purify the Seat.
Sprinkle water on your seat while chanting:

पृथ्वि त्वया धृता लोकाः देवि त्वं विष्णुना धृता।
त्वं च धारय मां देवि पवित्रं कुरु चासनम्।।

pṛthvi tvayā dhṛtā lokāḥ devi tvaṃ viṣṇunā dhṛtā
tvaṃ ca dhāraya māṃ devi pavitraṃ kuru cāsanam

O Mother Earth, all the worlds are held by you. You are held by *Viṣṇu*. May you hold me, O Goddess, and purify my seat.

6. *Ghaṇṭā pūjā* - Worship of the Bell to Purify the Atmosphere.
Ring the bell while chanting:

आगमार्थं तु देवानां गमनार्थं तु रक्षसाम्।
कुर्वे घण्टारवं तत्र देवताह्वानलाञ्छनम्।।

āgamārthaṃ tu devānaṃ gamanārthaṃ tu rakṣasām
kurve ghaṇṭaravaṃ tatra devatāhvānalāñchanam

For the arrival of the deities and for the departure of destructive forces, I ring the bell, marking the invocation of the deity.

7. *Kalaśa pūjā* - Worship of the Pot of Water to Purify all *pūjā* Materials.
Offer flowers in the *pañcapātram*, small pot, which has been filled with water and decorated with sandal paste and vermilion. Cover the *pañcapātram* with the right palm and chant:

गङ्गे च यमुने चैव गोदावरि सरस्वति।
नर्मदे सिन्धु कावेरि जलेऽस्मिन् सन्निधिं कुरु।।

gaṅge ca yamune caiva godāvari sarasvati
narmade sindhu kāveri jale'smin sannidhiṃ kuru

O Rivers *Gaṅgā, Yamunā, Godāvarī, Sarasvatī, Narmadā, Sindhu, Kāverī*, may you all be present in this water!

Sprinkle the water from the *pañcapātram* on all the *pūjā* materials and on oneself.

8. *Ātma pūjā* - Worship of the Self.

Fold hands and chant:

देहो देवालयः प्रोक्तः जीवो देवस्सनातनः।
त्यजेदज्ञाननिर्माल्यं सोऽहं भावेन पूजयेत्।।

deho devālayaḥ proktaḥ jīvo devassanātanaḥ
tyajedajñānanirmālyaṃ so'haṃ bhāvena pūjayet

The body is the temple. The *jīva* is the deity of this temple since the beginningless time. May one remove wilted flowers that are looked upon as ignorance and worship the Lord with an understanding that he is non-separate from oneself.

The Sixteen-step *Pūjā*:

1. *Āvāhanam* - Invocation

   Visualise the form of the deity and chant a *śloka* addressed to the deity. Take flowers and *akṣatas*, rice, in hand and after chanting, offer at the feet of the Lord.

   अस्मिन् बिम्बे श्री देवं (or the chosen deity) ध्यायामि।
   अस्मिन् बिम्बे श्री देवं (or the chosen deity) आवाहयामि।

   asmin bimbe śrī devaṃ (or the chosen deity) *dhyāyami*
   asmin bimbe śrī devaṃ (or the chosen deity) *āvāhayāmi*

   I visualise Lord *Deva*. I invoke his form in this image.

2. *Āsanam* - Seat

   Offer flowers at the feet of the Lord, chanting:

   आसनं समर्पयामि।

   āsanaṃ samarpayāmi

   O Lord! I offer you a seat.

3. *Pādyam* - Water for Washing the Feet.

   Offer water in a cup, chanting:

   पाद्यं समर्पयामि।

   pādyaṃ samarpayāmi

   O Lord! I offer you water for washing the feet.

4. *Arghyam* - Water for Washing the Hands.

   Offer water in a cup, chanting:

   अर्घ्यं समर्पयामि ।

   arghyaṃ samarpayāmi

   O Lord! I offer you water for washing the hands.

5. *Ācamanīyaṃ* - Water for Inner Purification.

   Offer water in a cup, chanting:

   आचमनीयं समर्पयामि।

   ācamanīyaṃ samarpayāmi

   O Lord! I offer you water for inner purification.

6. *Madhuparkam* - Sweet

   Offer water (or any offering such as ghee, curds, honey, or sugar) in a cup, chanting:

मधुपर्कं समर्पयामि ।

madhuparkaṃ samarpayāmi

O Lord! I offer you the sweet.

7. *Snānam* - Bath
   Offer water in a cup, chanting:

   स्नानं समर्पयामि ।

   snānaṃ samarpayāmi

   O Lord! I offer you a bath.

   Offer water in a cup, chanting:

   स्नानानन्तरम् आचमनीयं समर्पयामि।

   snānānantaram ācamanīyaṃ samarpayāmi

   After the bath, I offer you water for inner purification.

8. *Vastram* - Cloth
   Offer flowers or *akṣatas*, chanting:

   वस्त्रं समर्पयामि।

   vastraṃ samarpayāmi

   O Lord! I offer you cloth.

   उपवीतं समर्पयामि।

   upavītaṃ samarpayāmi

   O Lord! I offer you the sacred thread.

9. *Ābharaṇam* - Ornaments
   Offer flowers or *akṣatas*, chanting:

   आभरणं समर्पयामि।

   ābharaṇaṃ samarpayāmi

   O Lord! I offer you ornaments.

10. *Gandham* and *Kuṅkumam* - Sandalpaste and Vermilion.
    Offer flowers, *akṣatas* or sandalpaste, chanting:

    गन्धान् धारयामि।

    gandhān dhārayāmi

    O Lord! I offer you sandalpaste.

गन्धस्योपरि हरिद्राकुङ्क□ुमं समर्पयामि।

gandhasyopari haridrākuṅkumaṃ samarpayāmi

O Lord! I offer you vermilion over the sandalpaste.

11. *Puṣpam* - Flowers

Offer flowers, chanting:

पुष्पाणि समर्पयामि ।

puṣpāṇi samarpayāmi

O Lord! I offer you flowers.

One may chant "अष्टोत्तरशतनामावलिः" "*aṣṭottaraśatanāmāvaliḥ*", the one hundred and eight names of the Lord. With each name offer flowers.

12. *Dhūpam* - Incense

Show the incense to the Lord with circular clockwise motion three times; simultaneously ring the bell with the left hand, and chant:

धूपमाघ्रापयामि ।

dhūpamāghrāpayāmi

O Lord! I offer you incense.

13. *Dīpam* - Lamp

Show the lamp held in the right hand with a circular clockwise motion three times; simultaneously ring the bell with the left hand, and chant:

दीपं सन्दर्शयामि।

dīpaṃ sandarśayāmi

O Lord! I offer you this light.

Offer a spoon full of water in the cup, chanting:

धूपदीपानन्तरम् आचमनीयं समर्पयामि।

dhūpadīpānantaram ācamanīyaṃ samarpayāmi

O Lord! After *dhūpa* and *dīpa*, I offer you water.

14. *Naivedyam* - Food

a. Sprinkle water on the food while chanting:

ॐ भूर्भुवस्सुवः । ॐ तत्सवितुर्वरेण्यम् । भर्गो देवस्य धीमहि ।
धियो यो नः प्रचोदयात् ।

oṃ bhūrbhuvassuvaḥ oṃ tatsaviturvareṇyam bhargo devasya dīmahi
dhiyo yo naḥ pracodayāt

The three worlds are pervaded by the Lord, the creator. *om* is the basis of everything. That Lord is the one who is the most worshipful. We meditate on that all-knowing Lord. May he set our intellects in the right direction.

b. Ring the bell and offer the sanctified food with a flower in hand, with a sweeping motion from the food up towards the altar, for each of these six chants:

ॐ प्राणाय स्वाहा । अपानाय स्वाहा । ॐ व्यानाय स्वाहा ।
ॐ उदानाय स्वाहा । ॐ समानाय स्वाहा । ॐ ब्रह्मणे स्वाहा ।

oṃ prāṇāya svāhā. om apānāya svāhā. oṃ vyānāya svāhā.
oṃ udānāya svāhā. oṃ samānāya svāhā. oṃ brahmaṇe svāhā

I offer this to *prāṇa*. I offer this to *apāna*. I offer this to *vyāna*.
I offer this to *udāna*. I offer this to *samāna*. I offer this to the Lord.

c. Offer food at the feet of the Lord while chanting:

नैवेद्यं निवेदयामि।

naivedyaṃ nivedayāmi

O Lord! I offer you food.

d. Offer water while chanting:

नैवेद्यानन्तरम् आचमनीयं समर्पयामि।

naivedyānantaram ācamanīyaṃ samarpayāmi

O Lord! I offer you water after the food.

e. Offer betel leaves and nuts, chanting:

ताम्ब□ूलं समर्पयामि।

tāmbūlaṃ samarpayāmi

O Lord! I offer you betel leaves and nuts.

*(If you don't have *tāmbūlam* you may chant *tāmbūlārtham akṣatān samarpayāmi* and offer *akṣatās* instead).

15. *Karpūra-nīrājanam* - Lighted Camphor

a. Standing, show the camphor with circular clockwise motion three times; simultaneously ring the bell with the left hand and chant:

न तत्र सूर्यो भाति न चन्द्रतारकं
नेमा विद्युतो भान्ति कुतोयमग्निः।
तमेवभान्तमनुभाति सर्वं
तस्य भासा सर्वमिदं विभाति॥

na tatra sūryo bhāti na candratārakaṃ
nemā vidyuto bhānti kuto'yamagniḥ
tameva bhāntamanubhāti sarvaṃ
tasya bhāsā sarvamidaṃ vibhāti

There the sun does not shine, nor do the moon or stars. There this lightning does not shine; what to talk of this fire? That (awareness) shining, everything shines after it; by the light of that awareness, all this shines in various forms.

Offer lighted camphor, chanting:

कर्पूरनीराजनं सन्दर्शयामि ।

karpūranīrājanaṃ sandarśayāmi

O Lord! I show you lighted camphor.

b. Offer a spoonful of water into the cup while chanting:

आचमनीयं समर्पयामि ।

ācamanīyaṃ samarpayāmi

O Lord! I offer you water for inner purification.

16. *Vandanam* - Salutation

a. Continue standing and offer flowers, chanting:

मन्त्रपुष्पं समर्पयामि।

mantrapuṣpaṃ samarpayāmi

O Lord! I offer you flowers with sacred chants.

b. Turn around oneself three times clockwise while chanting the *mantras* given below:

यानि कानि च पापानि जन्मान्तरकृतानि च।
तानि तानि विनश्यन्ति प्रदक्षिण पदे पदे ॥

yāni kāni ca pāpāni janmāntarakṛtāni ca
tāni tāni vinaśyanti pradakṣiṇa pade pade

May those omissions and commissions done in this life and also in the previous births and the resulting afflictions perish with every *pradakṣiṇa*.

तव तत्वं न जानामि कीदृशोऽसि महेश्वर ।
यादृशोऽसि महादेव तादृशाय नमो नमः ॥

tava tatvaṃ na jānāmi kīdṛśo'si maheśvara
yādṛśo'si mahādeva tādṛśāya namo namaḥ

O Lord! what is your nature? I do not know your nature. Whatever be your nature, I offer salutations to you who are of that nature.

Offer salutations, chanting:

प्रदक्षिणनमस्कारान् समर्पयामि ।

pradakṣiṇanamaskārān samarpayāmi

O Lord! I offer you circumambulation and prostration.

c. To seek forgiveness, one may chant:

मन्त्रहीनं क्रियाहीनं भक्तिहीनं महेश्वर ।
यत्पूजितं मया देव परिपूर्णं तदस्तु ते ।।

mantrahīnam kriyāhīnaṃ bhaktihīnam maheśvara
yatpūjitaṃ mayā deva paripūrṇaṃ tadastute

O Lord! may the *pūjā* done by me, even though devoid of proper *mantras*, wanting in the steps and in devotion, be received by you as complete.

Release the deity by offering flowers and *akṣatas* at the altar and chant:

अस्माद् बिम्बाद् आवाहितं श्रीदेवं यथास्थानं प्रतिष्ठापयामि ।

asmād bimbād āvāhitaṃ śrīdevaṃ yathāsthānaṃ prathiṣṭāpayāmi

The Lord *Deva* (or the chosen deity) invoked at this altar is placed again in his own glory.

Samarpaṇam - Dedication to the Lord.

Take water in the right hand and pour the water in front of the deity while chanting:

कायेन वाचा मनसेन्द्रियैर्वा बुद्ध्यात्मना वा प्रकृतेस्स्वभावात्।
करोमि यद्यत्सकलं परस्मै नारायणायेति समर्पयामि ।।

kāyena vācā manasendriyairvā buddhyātmanā vā prakṛtessvabhāvāt
karomi yadyat sakalaṃ parasmai nārāyaṇāyeti samarpayāmi

Unto Lord *Nārāyaṇa*, I dedicate all the acts that I perform with my body, speech, mind, senses and intellect which are born of deliberation or natural tendencies.

Complete the *pūjā* with a salutation.

Take the water, flowers and *naivedya* as *prasāda* from the Lord.

Prayers

Prayers

INTRODUCTION

Prayer is the highest form of communication with the Lord, and can be offered in simple words or as an elaborate ritual. The modes of prayer may differ from person to person, but the attitude is fundamental to all. Prayer helps nurture one's special relationship to the Lord - the relationship of the created to the creator - by invoking the devotee in the person. Unlike the other relative roles one plays, the role of a devotee is non-demanding since the Lord seeks nothing from us. When one's relationship to the Lord becomes primary in life, other relationships become secondary and, thus, less problematic.

Prayer has its purpose in helping one achieve an object of desire, be it mental clarity or a given end. Ultimately, prayer helps one gain the maturity to be a qualified recipient of spiritual knowledge. This knowledge teaches us our identity with the Lord and helps us discover freedom and happiness, the nature of oneself.

In the creation of any object, two types of causes are necessary. One is an intelligent cause which has the knowledge and the skill to create the object, and the second is the material cause from which the object is created. The two causes may rest with one being or may be separate from each other. For example, the dreamer is both the intelligent and the material cause of the dream-creation, while the watchmaker is only the intelligent cause of the watch, the material being different than the watchmaker.

When one looks at the world, one sees intelligence and order in the creation. The sun stays in its position; the planets do not go out of their orbit; the laws of physics do not take a vacation. Every organism has its place, every cell has its meaningful function. Nothing is without purpose. This being so, there must be an intelligent and a material cause for this creation.

Now, do these two causes rest in one being or are they separate from each other? If one says that the material cause exists apart from the Lord, then the question would arise as to who created that separate material. If it were created by another Lord, then from what did he or she make the material? One would end up in infinite regression looking for the first material. And, where would the separate material exist before the creation of space? Time and space are themselves part of this creation. Therefore, the material cause cannot exist apart from the intelligent cause of the creation. In fact, the creation does not exist apart from the Lord. What exists is the Lord alone.

With this understanding, if one asks where the Lord exists in the creation, the answer is that the Lord exists everywhere. What is the Lord's form? It is all forms, since nothing exists separate from the Lord. If all forms are the Lord's form, then how does one worship the Lord? One can worship the Lord by invoking him in any given form.

Innumerable laws govern the creation. The Lord, seen from a given law or function, becomes the presiding deity of that law or function. For instance, the Lord seen from the function of creation is *Brahmā*, the presiding deity of creation. Similarly, from the standpoint of preservation and destruction, the Lord is the presiding deities *Viṣṇu* and *Śiva*, respectively. The presiding deity of the function of sight is *Sūrya*, the sun and so on. The presiding deities may be male or female principles, since creation is equally composed of both aspects. Thus, prayer to any deity is prayer to the Lord alone.

Three Types of Prayer

Prayer is expressed in three ways: physical, *kāyika*; oral, *vācika*; and mental, *mānasa*. A ritual or a *pūjā* is a physical form of prayer. Singing in praise of the Lord or chanting verses and Vedic hymns is an oral prayer. *Japa* or worship done silently is a mental prayer.

In this section on 'Prayers' we include a variety of chants which can be done orally.

The Results of Prayer

Like any other action, prayer produces a result. The result is twofold: one is immediately seen, *dṛṣṭa -phala* and the other is unseen, *adṛṣṭa-phala*.

The immediate result of prayer is the inner comfort that comes from acknowledging one's limited capacities and accepting a power higher than oneself. Being objective about situations over which one has no control and praying to that all-knowing source is an act that frees one from anxiety regarding the expectation of a result.

The unseen result of prayer refers to the subtle result called *puṇya*, which accrues to the doer of the action. *Puṇya* manifests in the form of comfortable situations whether in this life or later. When one prays for success, the accrued *puṇya*, which one may call 'grace', helps neutralise obstacles that one may not foresee. The 'grace' may not ensure success, but without it the outcome could be worse.

The Purpose of Prayer

A prayer may carry a different intent for different individuals. In the *Bhagavad Gītā*, Lord *Kṛṣṇa* describes four types of devotees. The first one is called an *ārtha*. This individual remembers the Lord only during crisis and difficulties. When things seem to be going fairly well, the *ārtha* attributes success to his efforts alone.

The second type of devotee is said to be an *arthārthī*. This is a religious person who is aware of the Lord's grace in his life, but whose motivation for prayer stems from seeking personal ends. The *arthārthī* is committed only to material gains and pleasures. Like the *ārtha*, he also prays for relief from distress.

The third type of devotee is a *jijñāsu*. This person pursues knowledge for *mokṣa*, freedom from unhappiness. Though *mokṣa* is a desirable end for all, only a *jijñāsu* recognises knowledge as the means to this end and pursues it. His prayer is for inner growth and maturity for the sake of gaining this knowledge.

The *jñānī* is the fourth type of devotee. This is a wise person who knows his identity with the Lord. In the *Bhagavad Gītā*, Lord *Kṛṣṇa* describes the wise person as being one with the Lord. The *jñānī's* prayer is an expression of wisdom, and is the highest form of prayer.

Invoking the Unknown Factor

There are three factors necessary in accomplishing an end. The first factor is adequate effort, *prayatna*. One cannot accomplish anything in life without adequate effort. The second factor is time, *kāla*. Once effort is made, time is necessary for the results to fructify. For example, when one sows a seed, time has to elapse for the plant to grow before it bears fruit. The length of time varies according to the nature of action and the result desired.

Despite making adequate effort and allowing sufficient time, the result may not always meet one's expectations. One's knowledge and power being limited, one cannot foresee and make things happen as one wants. There is always an unknown element, the third factor, often called chance or luck.

A person who is sensitive and acknowledges the presence of the Lord sees this third factor as *daivam*. Such a person knows that the Lord's laws govern the results of actions and, through prayer, the person invokes the grace of those laws for obtaining desired results. The laws being nonseparate from the Lord, prayer is efficacious in accomplishing a given end.

The Meaning of *Oṃkāra* and *Śānti*

Om is the name for *Brahman*, the cause and the basis of creation. *Om*, as a sound symbol, also indicates auspiciousness and is chanted at the beginning of prayers and religious studies. *Om* is derived from the Sanskrit verbal root '*av*', meaning 'to protect'. When one chants *om* with the understanding that it is a name for the Lord, it becomes a prayer for one's protection.

Om etymologically is composed of three sounds, '*a*', '*u*' and '*m*'. The first syllable, '*a*', stands for the waking world, the waker and the waking experience. The second syllable '*u*', stands for the dream world, the dreamer and the dream experience. The third syllable '*m*', stands for the sleep world, the sleeper and the sleep experience. As one chants *om* repeatedly, the silence between the chants (called *amātrā*) stands for the awareness, the consciousness which is the basis of the three worlds, the three experiencers and the three states of experience. *Om* thus represents all that exists and the basis or substratum of all that exists.

In any pursuit, including education, there can be a number of obstacles, *tāpas*. These obstacles fall into three categories:

1. *Ādhidaivika*

Obstacles which are natural and over which we have no control, e.g., storms, earthquakes, floods.

2. *Ādhibhautika*

Obstacles created by one's surroundings, e.g., noisy neighbours, traffic, distractions caused by one's family.

3. *Ādhyātmika*

Obstacles and distractions created within oneself, e.g., tiredness, an agitated or distracted mind.

Any of these obstacles can prevent one from achieving success in a given endeavour. *Śāntii* (peace) is, therefore, chanted three times for the mitigation and the removal of these threefold obstacles.

How to Chant the Prayers

Chanting Tape - An audio tape of the prayers accompanies this Teaching Programme. The tape is an instructional aid to help parents and teachers learn how to properly chant the prayers.

Pronunciation - To properly chant the Vedic prayers, an understanding of the Sanskrit letters and their pronunciation is necessary. Please see the 'Key to Transliteration' for pronunciation of the Sanskrit letters.

The pronunciation of a letter involves 1) a point of articulation and 2) effort.

1) The point of articulation refers to the place in the vocal apparatus which produces the specific sound. Letters are classified as gutturals, palatals, linguals, dentals and labials depending on their place of production, which range from back to front of the vocal apparatus.

2) Letters are classified as either voiced or unvoiced, aspirated or unaspirated, according to the effort involved. Voiced letters involve the vibration of the vocal cords; while unvoiced letters can be sounded without involving the vibration of the vocal cords, e.g., ग् (*g*) is voiced and क् (*k*) is unvoiced. An aspirated letter is pronounced by forcing air out while saying the latter. This is represented in transliteration by adding an '*h*' to the initial letter sound, e.g., क (*ka*) unaspirated and ख (*kha*) aspirated.

In the case of vowels, pronunciation is characterised by 1) duration 2) tone 3) nasalisation.

1) Duration is represented by units of time. Vowel duration may be short, long or prolated. For instance, the time required to pronounce उ (*u*) is short, one *mātrā*; ऊ (*ū*) is long, two *mātrās*, twice the duration of = . The prolated has the duration of three times of उ (*u*), three *mātrās*.

2) The three tones of voice used in Vedic chanting are: low, high and middle. For instance, in the Vedic chant सह नाववतु (*saha nāvavatu*) the अ (*a*) of स (*sa*) is low tone, the आ (*ā*) of ना (*nā*) is high tone and the remaining vowels are in the middle. Also, in स्वाहा (*svāhā*), the tone slides up from middle to high.

3) A vowel may be nasalised or non-nasalised in pronunciation, such as अं (*aṃ*) or अ (*a*). This nasalisation is represented by *anusvāra* (ं) above the vowel and its pronunciation is influenced by the consonant that follows.

Following definite rules of pronunciation, Vedic chanting has come down to us over hundreds of generations and, even today, Vedic prayers are chanted just as they were in ancient times.

Volume I * Part One

The *ślokas* introduced in Part One form a part of the sixteen-step *pūjā*. The sixteen-step *pūjā* will be introduced in its entire form in Part Three. The *ślokas* can also be recited individually as verses of prayer.

Volume I * Part Two

Part Two introduces additional *ślokas* that form a part of the sixteen-step *pūjā*. These *ślokās* can also be recited individually as prayer verses.

Volume I * Part Three

The peace invocation is for the elimination of all obstacles in one's pursuit of knowledge and may be recited before one begins one's scriptural studies. The welfare invocations are for the welfare of humanity and may be recited in the morning after a shower, or at the end of the day.

The prayer '*Kara Darśanam*' aids one to seek the Lord's blessings in all actions that are to be performed during the day. It may be chanted immediately after one gets up from the bed. *Bhūmi Namaskārah̤* chanted thereafter, seeks forgiveness for placing one's feet on *Bhūmi Devī*.

Also included are prayers to *Śrī Gaṇeśa*, *Śrī Śiva* and *Śrī Devī*.

Volume I * Part Four

The *Mṛtyuñjaya Mantra* is traditionally chanted for a person who is ill or approaching death.

The lamp prayer symbolises lighting the lamp of knowledge in our hearts. This act is significant when performed at the altar every day.

A prayer to Goddess *Sarasvatī* before studies is important to children, since education and learning are a major commitment at their stage of life.

Also included are prayers to *Śrī Sarasvatī*, *Śrī Viṣṇu* and *Śrī Lakṣmī*.

Volume I * Part Five

The peace indication is for seeking the blessings of various deities for the healthy functioning of the body-mind-sense complex.

To pray before eating one's meal is common in many cultures. It brings awareness of the many blessings one enjoys in life.

A prayer before sleep addresses the omissions and commissions of the day and asks forgiveness and wisdom from the Lord.

Also included are prayers to *Śrī Rāma*, *Śrī Kṛṣṇa* and *Śrī Hanumān*.

Volume II * Part Six

This part contains a set of prayers called *Guru-vandanam*, offering salutations to the teacher and the teaching tradition. These prayers are followed by prayers to Lord *Dakṣṇāmūrti*.

Lord *Dakṣṇāmūrti* is a manifestation of Lord *Śiva* in the form of a teacher, who, sitting under a banyan tree, unfolds the scriptures to his four disciples. These prayer verses, entitled *Dakṣṇāmūrti - dhyānaślokas*, are selected from *Dakṣṇāmūrti-stotram*, written by *Ādi Śaṅkara*. While offering salutations to Lord *Dakṣṇāmūrti*, the verses unfold the knowledge taught in the scriptures.

Next are the first and the last verses from *Gītā-dhyānam*. *Gītā-dhyānam* is a composition in praise of the *Bhagavad Gītā*, Lord *Kṛṣṇa* and Sage *Vyāsa*. It is written by *Śrī Madhusūdana Sarasvatī* and is traditionally recited before the study of the *Gītā*.

This section ends with verses twelve to twenty from the fifteenth chapter of the *Bhagavad Gītā*. In these verses, Lord *Kṛṣṇa* teaches *Arjuna* the fact that everything in creation, including the energy that nourishes all living beings, is the very Lord. These verses are traditionally chanted before eating.

Volume II * Part Seven

This part contains *stotras*, hymns, in praise of the Lord. The Sanskrit word '*stotra*' is derived from the root '*stu*' meaning 'to praise'.

The first *stotra* is *Śiva-pañcākṣara-stotra*. The *mantra* '*oṃ namaḥ śivāya*', is the essence of the *Śiva-pañcākṣara-stotra*. Each verse of the *stotra* represents one syllable of this *mantra*. The last verse gives the result obtained by the one who recites this hymn.

Gaṅgā-stotram, the second *stotra*, was composed by *Ādi Śaṅkara*. It is a hymn in praise of *Gaṅgā*, the perennial river, which symbolises the flow of knowledge coming down through the ages from teacher to student.

Volume II * Part Eight

This part begins with *Śāradā-stotram*, a hymn in praise of Goddess *Śāradā*, also known as Goddess *Sarasvatī*. One offers salutations to the Goddess and seeks her blessings in one's pursuit of knowledge.

Next are series of *Ārati-mantras*. The first *mantra* is in praise of *Kubera*, the presiding deity of wealth and prosperity. This *mantra* is followed by *Mantra-puṣpam*. The final prayer in this section reveals the meaning of the word *Om* as *Brahman*.

Volume II * Part Nine

The first set of verses in this part is called *Prātaḥ-smaraṇam.* These verses, attributed to *Ādi Śaṅkara* are chanted early in the morning. They are contemplative verses, in the form of a prayer, which reveal the nature of the self.

Next are the *Śānti-mantras*, invocatory prayers for peace, drawn from various *Upaniṣads.* These *mantras* are to be recited in a specified manner with the correct *svaras*, intonations.

Volume III * Part Ten

Ādityahṛdaya Stotra is a prayer addressed to the sun deity for the elimination of mental weariness and gain of fortitude. *Śrī Rāma* chanted this prayer and was successful in destroying *Rāvaṇa.* Lord Sun is also worshipped for healthy eyes.

Śrī Annapūrṇā Stotra glorifies Goddess *Pārvatī* as *Śakti*, the power which blesses also with desired ends. One chants these verses seeking food for the physical body as well as food for the mind, viz., knowledge.

Volume III * Part Eleven

Śrī Nāma Rāmāyaṇa is a composition depicting the story of Lord *Rāma* in simple phrases in Sanskrit. It is chanted daily invoking the grace of Lord *Rāma*.

Śrī Hanumān Cālīsā is a prayer widely known in Northern India. This prayer is in praise of Lord *Hanumān.* It is believed that one accomplishes one's desired aims chanting this *stotra* for a specific period viz., one *maṇḍala* (40 days).

Volume III * Part Twelve

Bhagavad Gītā Dhyānaślokas are prayer verses chanted before reciting any chapter of the *Gītā.* These verses are in praise of *Bhagavad Gītā,* Lord *Kṛṣṇa* and *Veda Vyāsa.*

Bhagavad Gītā Chapter 2 is the subject of the tenth year teaching programme. Word-to-word meanings and translations are available in the tenth part of the teaching manual.

Nirvāṇaṣaṭka is a prayer consisting of six meditative verses dealing with contemplation upon the self. In the vision of the scriptures, the self is revealed as limitless pure awareness. These verses are meant to discover and abide in the true nature of the self as unfolded by the scriptures.

The eight *ślokas* are introduced in this section. These are chanted along with other *ślokas* while performing a sixteen-step *pūjā*.

1. Offer flowers chanting:

दीपज्योतिः परं ब्रह्म दीपज्योतिर्जनार्दनः।
दीपो मे हरतु पापं दीपज्योतिर्नमोऽस्तुते॥

dīpajyotiḥ paraṃ brahma dīpajyotir janārdanaḥ
dīpo me haratu pāpaṃ dīpajyotir namo stute

The light of the lamp stands for *Brahman*, the unmanifest truth as well as for Lord *Viṣṇu* (in his manifest form). Let that light of lamp remove my *pāpas* results of omissions and commissions.

2. *Guru Dhyānam* - Visualisation of one's *Guru*.

गुरुर्ब्रह्मा गुरुर्विष्णुः गुरुर्देवो महेश्वरः ।
गुरुस्साक्षात् परं ब्रह्म तस्मै श्रीगुरवे नमः।

gururbrahmā gururviṣṇuḥ gururdevo maheśvaraḥ
gurussākṣāt paraṃ brahma tasmai śrī gurave namaḥ

The *guru* is *Brahmā*, the *guru* is *Viṣṇu*, the *guru* is *Maheśvara*. The *guru* is ultimate truth. Unto that *guru* my prostration.

3. *Vighneśvara Dhyānam* - Visualisation of Lord *Gaṇeśa*.

Lightly tap the temples with the knuckles, chanting the following *mantra*:

शुक्लाम्बरधरं विष्णुं शशिवर्णं चतुर्भुजम्।
प्रसन्नवदनं ध्यायेत् सर्वविघ्नोपशान्तये॥

śuklāmbaradharaṃ viṣṇuṃ śaśivarṇaṃ caturbhujam
prasannavadanaṃ dhyāyet sarvavighnopaśāntaye

May one meditate upon Lord *Vighneśvara*, who wears the white garment, who is all pervasive, who has a bright complexion (like the full moon), who has four hands (representing all power), who has an ever-smiling face (or an elephant face), for the removal of all obstacles.

4. *Āsana pūjā* - Worship of the Earth to Purify the Seat.

Sprinkle water on your seat while chanting:

पृथ्वि त्वया धृता लोकाः देवि त्वं विष्णुना धृता।
त्वं च धारय मां देवि पवित्रं कुरु चासनम्॥

pṛthvi tvayā dhṛtā lokāḥ devi tvaṃ viṣṇunā dhṛtā
tvaṃ ca dhāraya māṃ devi pavitraṃ kuru cāsanam

O Mother Earth, all the worlds are held by you. You are held by *Viṣṇu*. May you hold me, O Goddess, and purify my seat.

5. *Ghaṇṭā pūjā* - Worship of the Bell to Purify the Atmosphere.

Ring the bell while chanting:

आगमार्थं तु देवानां गमनार्थं तु रक्षसाम्।
कुर्वे घण्टारवं तत्र देवताह्वानलाञ्छनम्॥

āgamārthaṃ tu devānaṃ gamanārthaṃ tu rakṣasām
kurve ghaṇṭaravaṃ tatra devatāhvānalāñchanam

For the arrival of the deities and for the departure of destructive forces, I ring the bell, marking the invocation of the deity.

6. *Kalaśa pūjā* - Worship of the Pot of Water to Purify all *pūjā* Materials.

Offer flowers in the *pañcapātram*, small pot, which has been filled with water and decorated with sandal paste and vermilion. Cover the *pañcapātram* with the right palm and chant:

गङ्गे च यमुने चैव गोदावरि सरस्वति।
नर्मदे सिन्धु कावेरि जलेऽस्मिन् सन्निधिं कुरु॥

gaṅge ca yamune caiva godāvari sarasvati
narmade sindhu kāveri jale'smin sannidhiṃ kuru

O Rivers *Gaṅgā*, *Yamunā*, *Godāvarī*, *Syarasvatī*, *Narmadā*, *Sindhu*, *Kāverī*, may you all be present in this water!

Sprinkle the water from the *pañcapātram* on all the *pūjā* materials and on oneself.

7. *Ātma pūjā* - Worship of the Self.

Fold hands and chant:

देहो देवालयः प्रोक्तः जीवो देवस्सनातनः।
त्यजेदज्ञाननिर्माल्यं सोऽहं भावेन पूजयेत्।।

deho devālayaḥ proktaḥ jīvo devassanātanaḥ
tyajedajñānanirmālyaṃ so'haṃ bhāvena pūjayet

The body is the temple. The *jīva* is the deity of this temple since the beginningless time. May one remove wilted flowers that are looked upon as ignorance and worship the Lord with an understanding that he is non-separate from oneself.

8. सरस्वति नमस्तुभ्यं वरदे कामरूपिणी।
विद्यारम्भं करिष्यामि सिद्धिर्भवतु मे सदा।।

sarasvati namastubhyaṃ varade kāmarūpiṇī
vidyārambhaṃ kariṣyāmi siddhirbhavatu me sadā

Salutation to you O Goddess *Sarasvati*, who is a giver of boons, and who has a beautiful form! I begin my studies. Let there be success for me always.

The five *slokas* are introduced in this section. These are chanted along with other *slokas* while performing a sixteen-step *pūjā*

1. *Karpūra-nīrājanam* - Lighted Camphor

   a. Standing, show the camphor with circular clockwise motion three times; simultaneously ring the bell with the left hand and chant:

   न तत्र सूर्यो भाति न चन्द्रतारकं
   नेमा विद्युतो भान्ति कुतोऽयमग्निः।
   तमेवभान्तमनुभाति सर्वं
   तस्य भासा सर्वमिदं विभाति॥

   na tatra sūryo bhāti na candratārakaṃ
   nemā vidyuto bhānti kuto'yamagniḥ
   tameva bhāntamanubhāti sarvaṃ
   tasya bhāsā sarvamidaṃ vibhāti

   There the sun does not shine, nor do the moon or stars. There this lightning does not shine; what to talk of this fire? That (awareness) shining, everything shines after it; by the light of that awareness, all this shines in various forms.

2. Turn around oneself three times clockwise while chanting the *mantras* given below:

   यानि कानि च पापानि जन्मान्तरकृतानि च।
   तानि तानि विनश्यन्ति प्रदक्षिण पदे पदे ॥

yāni kāni ca pāpāni janmāntarakṛtāni ca
tāni tāni vinaśyanti pradakṣiṇa pade pade

May those omissions and commissions done in this life and also in the previous births and the resulting afflictions perish with every *pradakṣiṇa*.

3. तव तत्वं न जानामि कीदृशोऽसि महेश्वर ।
यादृशोऽसि महादेव तादृशाय नमो नमः ॥

tava tatvaṃ na jānāmi kīdṛśo'si maheśvara
yādṛśo'si mahādeva tādṛśāya namo namaḥ

Lord! what is your nature? I do not know your nature. Whatever be your nature, I offer salutations to you who are of that nature.

4. To seek forgiveness, one may chant:

मन्त्रहीनं क्रियाहीनं भक्तिहीनं महेश्वर ।
यत्पूजितं मया देव परिपूर्णं तदस्तु ते॥

mantrahīnam kriyāhīnaṃ bhaktihīnam maheśvara
yatpūjitaṃ mayā deva paripūrṇaṃ tadastute

O Lord! may the *pūjā* done by me, even though devoid of proper *mantras*, wanting in the steps and in devotion, be received by you as complete.

5. *Samarpaṇam* - Dedication to the Lord.

Take water in the right hand and pour the water in front of the deity while chanting:

कायेन वाचा मनसेन्द्रियैर्वा बुद्ध्यात्मना वा प्रकृतेस्स्वभावात्।
करोमि यद्यत्सकलं परस्मै नारायणायेति समर्पयामि॥

kāyena vācā manasendriyairvā buddhyātmanā vā prakṛtessvabhāvāt
karomi yadyatsakalaṃ parasmai nārāyaṇāyeti samarpayāmi

Unto Lord *Nārāyaṇa*, I dedicate all the acts that I perform with my body, speech, mind, senses and intellect which are born of deliberation or natural tendencies.

Śānti Pāṭhaḥ - 1

ॐ स॒ ह ना॑ववतु। स॒ ह नौ॑ भुनक्तु ।
स॒ह वी॒र्यं॑ करवावहै । तेजस्विना॒वधी॑तमस्तु ।
मा वि॑द्विषा॒वहै॒ ॥ ॐ शान्तिः॒ शान्तिः॒ शान्तिः॒॥

oṃ sa ha nāvavatu / sa ha nau bhunaktu
saha vīryaṃ karavāvahai / tejasvināvadhītamastu
mā vidviṣāvahai oṃ śāntiḥ śāntiḥ śāntiḥ

Sanskrit to English Word Meaning

saḥ - he; *ha* - indeed; *nau* - both of us; *avatu* - may protect; *saḥ* - he; *ha* - indeed; *nau* - both of us; *bhunaktu* - may nourish; *saha* - together; *vīryaṃ karavāvahai* - may we acquire the capacity (to study and understand the scriptures); *tejasvi* - brilliant; *nau* - for us; *adhītam* - what is studied; *astu* - let it be; *mā vidviṣāvahai* - may we not disagree with each other; *oṃ śāntiḥ śāntiḥ śāntiḥ* - om peace, peace, peace

Translation

May the Lord indeed, protect both of us. May he indeed, nourish both of us. May we together acquire the capacity (to study and understand the scriptures). May our study be brilliant. May we not disagree with each other. *om* peace, peace, peace.

Brief Explanation

At the beginning of a class, the teacher and students generally recite this peace invocation together. Both seek the Lord's blessings for a study that is free of obstacles, such as poor memory, or the inability to concentrate, or poor health. They also seek blessings for a conducive relationship, without which communication of any subject matter is difficult. Therefore, this prayer is important for both the teacher and the student. (This prayer should be learned and recited using the three *svaras*, tones that are used in Vedic chanting.)

Svasti Pāṭhaḥ

स्वस्ति प्रजाभ्यः परिपालयन्ताम् । न्याय्येन मार्गेण महीं महीशाः ।
गोब्राह्मणेभ्यश्शुभमस्तु नित्यम् । लोकास्समस्तास्सुखिनो भवन्तु।।

svasti prajābhyaḥ paripālayantām / nyāyyena mārgeṇa mahīṃ mahīśāḥ
gobrāmaṇebhyaśśubhamastu nityam / lokāssamasthāssukhino bhavantu

Sanskrit to English Word Meaning

svasti - may there be happiness; *prajābhyaḥ* - for all people; *paripālayantām* - may rule; *nyāyyena* - by righteous; *mārgeṇa* - by means; *mahīṃ* - the earth; *mahīśāḥ* - rulers; *gobrāmaṇebhyaḥ* - for cows and men of wisdom; *śubham* - welfare; *astu* - may there be; *nityam* - at all times; *lokāḥ*- beings; *samasthāḥ* - all; *sukhinaḥ* - happy; *bhavantu* - be

Translation

May there be happiness for all people. May the rulers righteously rule the earth. May there be welfare for cows and men of wisdom at all times. May all beings be happy.

काले वर्षतु पर्जन्यः । पृथिवी सस्यशालिनी ।
देशोऽयं क्षोभरहितः । ब्राह्मणास्सन्तु निर्भयाः

kāle varṣatu parjanyaḥ / pṛthivī sasyaśālinī /
deśo'yaṃ kṣobharahitaḥ / brāhmaṇāssantu nirbhayāḥ

Sanskrit to English Word Meaning

kāle - at the proper time; *varṣatu* - may rain; *parjanyaḥ* - clouds; *pṛthivī* - earth; *sasya-śālinī* (*bhavatu*) - (be) producer of grains; *ayam* - this; *deśaḥ* - country; *kṣobha-rahitaḥ* (*bhavatu*) - (be) free from famine; *brāhmaṇāḥ*- men of wisdom; *santu* - be; *nirbhayāḥ* - fearless

Translation

May the clouds rain at the proper time. May the earth produce grains. May this country be free from famine. May men of wisdom be fearless.

सर्वे भवन्तु सुखिनः। सर्वे सन्तु निरामयाः
सर्वे भद्राणि पश्यन्तु। मा कश्चिद् दुःखभाग् भवेत् ॥

sarve bhavantu sukhinaḥ / sarve santu nirāmayāḥ /
sarve bhadrāṇi paśyantu / mā kaścid duḥkhabhāg bhavet

Sanskrit to English Word Meaning

sarve - all; *bhavantu* - may be; *sukhinaḥ* - happy; *sarve* - all; *santu* - may be; *nirāmayāḥ* - free from disease; *sarve* - all; *bhadrāṇi* - prosperity; *paśyantu* - may enjoy; *mā* - not; *kaścit* - anybody; *duḥkhabhāg* - one who experiences sorrow; *bhavet* - may be

Translation

May all be happy. May all be free from disease. May all enjoy prosperity. May none experience sorrow.

असतो मा सद्गमय । तमसो मा ज्योतिर्गमय ।
मृत्योर्मा अमृतं गमय ॥ ॐ शान्तिः शान्तिः शान्तिः ॥

asato mā sadgamaya / tamaso mā jyotirgamaya
mṛtyormā amṛtaṃ gamaya / oṃ śāntiḥ śāntiḥ śāntiḥ

Sanskrit to English Word Meaning

asatah - from unreal; *mā* - me; *sad* - to the real; *gamaya* - lead; *tamasah* - from darkness; *mā* - me; *jyotih* - to light; *gamaya* - lead; *mṛtyoh*- from death; *mā* - me; *amṛtam* - to immortality; *gamaya* - lead; *oṃ śāntiḥ śāntiḥ śāntiḥ* - *om* peace, peace, peace

Translation

Lead me (by giving knowledge) from the unreal to the real; from darkness (of ignorance) to light (of knowledge); from death (sense of limitation) to immortality (limitlessness, liberation). *Om* peace, peace, peace.

Brief Explanation

These are prayers for the prosperity and welfare of all humanity. To achieve anything in life, one has to make an effort and await the results. In addition, many unknown factors and laws influence the outcome of that effort. By praying to the Lord one acknowledges these laws as the natural order inseparable from the Lord, and one acknowledges the Lord as the giver of all results of actions. Finally, the last prayer is from a seeker committed to a life of truth, seeking knowledge and freedom.

Kara Darśanam

कराग्रे वसते लक्ष्मीः करमध्ये सरस्वती ।
करमूले स्थिता गौरी प्रभाते करदर्शनम् ॥

karāgre vasate lakṣmīḥḥ karamadhye sarasvatī
karamūle sthitā gaurī ḥ prabhāte karadarśanam

Sanskrit to English Word Meaning

karāgre - on the tip of your hand (palm); *vasate* - dwells; *lakṣmīḥ* - the Goddess of Prosperity, *Lakṣmī*; *kara-madhye* - in the middle of your hand (palm); *sarasvatī* - the Goddess of Knowledge, *Sarasvatī*; *karamūle* - on the base of your hand (palm); *sthitā* - abiding; *gaurī* - Goddess *Pārvatī*; *prabhāte* - in the morning; *kara-darśanam* - looking at your hand (palm)

Translation

On the forepart of your palm is Goddess *Lakṣmī*; in the middle of your palm is Goddess *Sarasvatī*; on the base of your palm is Goddess *Pārvatī*. In this manner, look at your palm in the morning.

Brief Explanation

This is a morning prayer called '*kara-darśanam*'. One begins the day with this prayer. '*Kara*' means the forearm including the palm. Here, *kara* refers to the palm of the hand and it stands for the five *karmendriyas* or the organs of action. While looking at the palm, one invokes the Lord in the form of various deities, thus sanctifying all the actions that will be done during the day. By acknowledging the Lord as the giver of the capacity to perform actions and as the giver of the fruits of those actions one sanctifies the action.

Bhūmi Namaskāraḥ

समुद्रवसने देवि पर्वतस्तनमण्डले।
विष्णुपत्नि नमस्तुभ्यं पादस्पर्शं क्षमस्व मे ॥

samudravasane devi parvatastanamandale
visnupatni namastubhyam pādasparśaṃ kṣamasva me

Sanskrit to English Word Meaning

samudravasane - O one who dwells in the ocean!; *devi* - the effulgent one!; *parvata-stana-mandale* - one whose breasts are big like the moutain and rounded; *visnupatni* - wife of Lord *Visnu*; *namaḥ* - (my) salutation; *tubhyam* - to you; *pādasparśam*- for my touching (you) with (my) feet; *kṣamasva* - forgive; *me* - me

Translation

O one who dwells in the ocean! the effulgent one! one whose breasts are big like the mountain and rounded, (my) salutation to you. Forgive me for my touching (you) with (my) feet.

Brief Explanation

This prayer is chanted after *kara-darśanam* when one places one's feet on Mother Earth for the first time at dawn. In the Vedic culture, Mother Earth is looked upon as Goddess, and not merely one of the five elements of creation. Therefore, placing one's feet on her is looked upon as an act of disrespect. In seeking forgiveness from the Goddess, one acknowledges the divinity around.

Śrī Gaṇeśaḥ

शुक्लाम्बरधरं विष्णुं शशिवर्णं चतुर्भुजम्।
प्रसन्नवदनं ध्यायेत् सर्वविघ्नोपशान्तये॥

śuklāmbaradaraṃ viṣṇuṃ śaśivarṇaṃ caturbhujam
prasannavadanaṃ dhyāyet sarvavighnopaśāntaye

Sanskrit to English Word Meaning

śuklāmbaradaram- one who wears the white garment; *viṣṇum* - who is all-pervading; *śaśi-varṇaṃ* - who has a bright complexion; *caturbhujam* - who has four hands; *prasanna-vadanam* - who has an ever-smiling face (or an elephant face); *dhyāyet* - may one meditate upon; *sarva-vighna-upaśāntaye* - for the removal of all obstacles

Translation

May one meditate upon Lord *Vighneśvara*, who wears the white garment, who is all pervasive, who has a bright complexion (like the full moon), who has four hands (representing all power), who has an ever-smiling face (or an elephant face), for the removal of all obstacles.

Brief Explanation

Lord *Gaṇeśa* is the older son of Lord *Śiva* and his consort, *Pārvatī*. The younger son is Lord *Kārtikeya*. Lord *Gaṇeśa* is invoked before any undertaking for the removal of obstacles. He is also worshipped for knowledge and wisdom he bestows upon devotees.

Śrī Śivaḥ

नम॑स्ते अस्तु भगवन् विश्वेश्व॒राय॑ महादे॒वाय॑ त्र्यम्ब॒काय॑ त्रिपुरान्त॒काय॑
त्रिकालाग्निका॒लाय॑ कालाग्निरु॒द्राय॑ नीलक॒ण्ठाय॑ मृत्युञ्ज॒याय॑
सर्वेश्व॒राय॑ सदाशि॒वाय॑ श्रीमन्महादे॒वाय॒ नमः॑

namaste astu bhagavan viśveśvarāya mahādevāya tryambakāya
tripurāntakāya trikālāgnikālaya kālāgnirudrāya nīlakaṇṭhāya
mṛtyuñjayāya sarveśvarāya sadāśivāya śrīmanmahādevāya namaḥ

Sanskrit to English Word Meaning

namaḥ - salutation; *te* - to you; *astu* - let it be; *bhagavan* - O Lord; *viśveśvarāya* - the master of the universe; *mahādevāya* - great Lord; *tryambakāya* - the three-eyed one; *tripurāntakāya* - the destroyer of *Tripura*; *trikālāgni-kālaya* - the extinguisher of the *Trikāla* fire; *kālāgnirudrāya* - the extinguisher of the fire of death; *nīlakaṇṭhāya* - the blue-necked one; *mṛtyuñjayāya* - the victor over death; *sarveśvarāya* - the Lord of all; *sadāśivāya* - the ever-auspicious one; *śrīman mahā devāya* - the glorious Lord of all deities; *namaḥ* - salutation

Translation

Salutation to you, O Lord, the master of the universe, the great Lord, the three-eyed one, the destroyer of *Tripura*, the extinguisher of the *Trikāla* fire and the fire of death, the blue-necked one, the victor over death, the Lord of all, the ever-auspicious one, the glorious Lord of all deities.

Brief Explanation

This Vedic prayer is taken from *Rudram*, which is a hymn to Lord *Śiva*. *Śiva* is the presiding deity of the function of destruction. The word '*Śiva*' means 'the auspicious one'. *Śiva's* third-eye symbolises wisdom, that wisdom by which *adharma* is destroyed and the apparent limitation of mortality is overcome. (This prayer should be learned and recited using the three *svaras*, tones that are used in Vedic chanting.)

Śrī Devī

सर्वमङ्गल माङ्गल्ये शिवे सर्वार्थसाधके
शरण्ये त्र्यम्बके गौरि नारायणि नमोऽस्तुते

sarvamangala māngalye śive sarvārthasādhake
śaraṇye tryambake gauri nārāyaṇi namo'stu te

Sanskrit to English Word Meaning

sarva-mangala-māngalye - the one who is the auspiciousness of all that is auspicious; *śive* - the consort of *Śiva*; *sarvārthasādhake* - who is the means of accomplishing all desires; *śaraṇye* - who is the refuge of all; *tryambake* - the three-eyed one; *gauri* - the fair-complexioned one; *nārāyaṇi* - O *Devī*; *namaḥ* - salutation; *astu* - let it be; *te* - to you

Translation

Salutation to you, O *Devī*, who is the auspiciousness of all that is auspicious, who is the consort of Lord *Śiva*, who is the means of accomplishing all desires, who is the refuge of all, who is three-eyed and who is the fair-complexioned one.

Brief Explanation

Goddess *Pārvatī* is the consort of Lord *Śiva* and is worshipped as *Śakti*. The puranic literature describes her as having many forms, including *Durgā*, *Caṇḍī*, *Kālī* and *Umā*. While *Śiva* represents the efficient cause of creation, *Śakti* symbolises the material cause.

Volume I * **Prayers** * Part 4

Mṛtyuñjaya Mantraḥ

ॐ त्र्यम्बकं यजामहे सुगन्धिं पुष्टिवर्धनम्।
उर्वारुकमिव बन्धनान्मृत्योर्मुक्षीय माऽमृतात्॥

oṃ tryambakaṃ yajāmahe sugandhim puṣṭivardhanam
urvārukamiva bandanānmṛtyormukṣīya mā'mṛtāt

Sanskrit to English Word Meaning

tryambakam - three-eyed (*Śiva*); *yajāmahe* - we offer our worship; *sugandhim* - fragrant; *puṣṭivardhanam* - one who enhances prosperity; *urvārukam* - the water melon; *iva* - like; *bandanāt* - from the bondage; *mṛtyoḥ* - of death; *mukṣīya* - liberate; *mā* - not; *amṛtāt* - from immortality

Translation

We offer our worship to the fragrant, three-eyed Lord *Śiva* who enhances prosperity. May he liberate us from the bondage of death like the water melon (which effortlessly separates from the vine); may he not (let us turn away) from immortality.

Brief Explanation

This *mantra* is taken from *Rudram*, which is a hymn on Lord *Śiva*. It is also called *mṛtyuñjaya-mantra*, meaning, it invokes the grace of Lord *Śiva* for conquering death.

This verse contains a beautiful metaphor. The *urvāruka* fruit is a melon which grows on the ground attached to a vine. It takes its time to ripen. When fully ripe, it does not have to be plucked. It detaches itself effortlessly, remaining where it is, but free from the vine. *Amṛta* is total freedom from the sense of all inadequacy and limitation. An essential requirement in gaining *amṛta* is emotional maturity, which is gained by the process of inner growth, by living a life of values and prayer. This maturing of the mind is likened to the ripening of the fruit.

There is another important aspect of this example. Freedom being the essential nature of the self, the mature mind does not have to seek outside itself to gain this freedom. When a mature mind is exposed to the teaching, it effortlessly comes to recognise that freedom. This is the gain of that which already has been gained. Thus, this is a prayer of a *mumukṣu*, a person who desires that total freedom and who makes it his main pursuit in life. It is also a *mantra* which is traditionally chanted by family and friends for a person who is ill or approaching death. (This prayer should be learned and recitied using the three *svaras*, tones that are used in Vedic chanting.)

Dīpa Darśanam

शुभं करोति कल्याणम् आरोग्यं धनसम्पदः
शत्रुबुद्धिविनाशाय दीपज्योतिर्नमोऽस्तुते ।

śubhaṃ karoti kalyāṇam ārogyaṃ dhanasampadaḥ
śatrubuddhivināśāya dīpajyotirnamo'stu te

Sanskrit to English Word Meaning

śubham - auspiciousness; *karoti* - which brings; *kalyāṇam* - prosperity; *ārogyam* - good health; *dhana-sampadaḥ*- abundance of wealth; *śatru-buddhi-vināśāya* - for the destruction of the intellect's enemy (ignorance); *dīpa-jyotiḥ* - that lamplight; *namaḥ* - salutation; *astu* - let it be; *te* - to you

Translation

The lamplight brings auspiciousness, prosperity, good health and abundance of wealth. Let (my) salutations be to you for the destruction of the ignorance which is the intellect's enemy.

Brief Explanation

This prayer is chanted before lighting the lamp. Light is considered a symbol of auspiciousness, prosperity and abundance in many cultures. Light brings with it brightness, but how does it destroy the intellect's enemy? The intellect's enemy is considered to be ignorance; its archenemy is self-ignorance. Ignorance is likened to darkness; knowledge is likened to light. A room may be full of objects and one's sight may be sharp, but if the room is in darkness, the objects cannot be perceived. Light removes the darkness and makes it possible to see the objects. In the same manner, the self (subject) is ever present in one's experiences, but due to ignorance, its essential nature is not known. As light removes darkness, knowledge of the self removes ignorance and allows one to discover happiness as the essential nature of the self.

Adhyayanāt Prāk

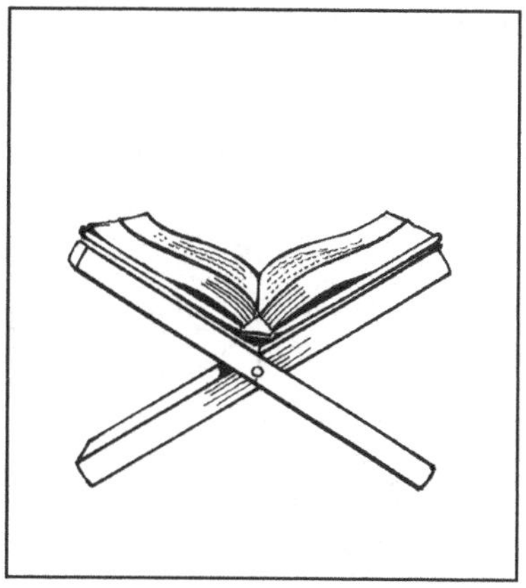

सरस्वति नमस्तुभ्यं वरदे काम रूपिणि।
विद्यारम्भं करिष्यामि सिद्धिर्भवतु मे सदा॥

sarasvati namastubhyaṃ varade kāmarūpiṇi
vidyārambham kariṣyāmi siddhirbhavatu me sadā

Sanskrit to English Word Meaning

sarasvati - O Goddess of Knowledge, *sarasvatī*; *namaḥ* - salutations; *tubhyam* - to you; *varade* - one who gives boons; *kāmarūpiṇi* - one who has a beautiful form; *vidyārambham* - the beginning of studies; *kariṣyāmi* - I do; *siddhiḥ* - success; *bhavatu* - may there be; *me* - for me; *sadā* - always

Translation

Salutations to you, O Goddess *Sarasvatī*, who is the giver of boons, and who has a beautiful form! I begin my studies. Let there be success for me always.

Brief Explanation

This prayer is chanted before studies. It is addressed to Goddess Sarasvat" who symbolises all forms of knowledge, including knowledge of the fine and performing arts. Knowledge is a fundamental pursuit of human life, and a life of study and learning provides nourishment and discipline to the human intellect. In the Vedic culture, study is considered one's duty. A Vedic mandate says, "*svādhyāyo'dhyetavyaḥ*" - may one study one's recension of *Veda*. Goddess *Sarasvatī*, is addressed as one who grants boons and fulfills desires. This prayer is chanted before beginning a class or at the beginning of one's study so that all learning may resolve in knowledge alone.

Śrī Sarasvatī

या देवी स्तूयते नित्यं विबुधैर्वेदपारगैः।
सा मे वसतु जिह्वाग्रे ब्रह्मरूपा सरस्वती॥

yā devī stūyate nityaṃ vibhudhairvedapāragaiḥ
sā me vasatu jihvāgre brahmarūpā sarasvatī

Sanskrit to English Word Meaning

yā - who; *devī* - the Goddess; *stūyate* - is praised; *nityam* - ever; *vibhudhair* - by the wise; *veda-pāragaiḥ* - those who have mastered the *Vedas*; *sā* - she; *me* - my; *vasatu* - may live; *jihvāgre* - on the tip of the tongue; *brahmarūpā* - the embodiment of the *Vedas* (or the consort of Lord *Brahmā*); *sarasvatī* - the Goddess of Knowledge

Translation

May *Sarasvatī*, the Goddess of Knowledge, who is ever praised by the wise who have mastered the scriptures, who is the embodiment of the *Vedas* (or the consort of Lord *Brahmā*), live on the tip of my tongue.

Brief Explanation

Goddess *Sarasvatī* is the consort of Lord *Brahmā*, the creator, and is the giver of all knowledge and wisdom. She is worshipped by students and seekers so that they may be blessed with brilliance, talent and knowledge.

Śrī Viṣṇuḥ

नमस्समस्तभूतानाम् आदिभूताय भूभृते ।
अनेकरूपरूपाय विष्णवे प्रभविष्णवे ।।

namassamastabhūtānām ādibhūtāya bhūbhṛte
anekarūparūpāya viṣṇave prabhaviṣṇave

Sanskrit to English Word Meaning

namaḥ - salutation; *samasta-bhūtānām* - of all the beings; *ādi-bhūtāya* - to the creator; *bhūbhṛte* - the sustainer of the creation; *aneka-rūpa-rūpāya* - the one whose form is all forms; *viṣṇave* - who is all pervasive; *prabha-viṣṇave* - the self-effulgent one

Translation

Salutation to Lord *Viṣṇu*, who is the creator of all beings, the sustainer of the creation, whose form is all forms, who is all pervasive, and who is self-effulgent.

Brief Explanation

Lord *Viṣṇu* is the presiding deity for all that sustains the creation. He is worshipped for prosperity and health.

Śrī Lakṣmīḥ

नमस्तेऽस्तु महामाये श्रीपीठे सुरपूजिते।
शङ्खचक्रगदाहस्ते महालक्ष्मी नमोऽस्तु ते॥

namaste'stu mahāmāye śrīpīṭhe surapūjite
śaṅkhacakragadāhaste mahālakṣmi namo'stu te

Sanskrit to English Word Meaning

namaḥ - salutation; *te* - unto you; *astu* - let it be; *mahāmāye* - who is all powers; *śrīpīṭhe* - who is the seat of wealth; *sura-pūjite* - who is worshipped by the gods; *śaṅkha-cakra-gadā-haste* - the one who wields a shell, a disc and a mace in her hands; *mahālakṣmi* - O Goddess of prosperity; *namaḥ* - salutation; *astu* - let it be; *te* - to you

Translation

Salutation to you, O *Mahālakṣmī*, who is all power, who is the seat of wealth, who is worshipped by the gods and who has a shell, a disc and a mace in her hands.

Brief Explanation

Goddess *Lakṣmī* is the consort of Lord *Viṣṇu.* Sustenance of anything requires wealth and resources. *Śrī Lakṣmī* blesses the creation with wealth, thereby supporting and sustaining the world.

Volume I * **Prayers** * Part 5

Śānti Pāṭhaḥ - 2

ॐ शन्नो मित्रः शं वरुणः। शन्नो भवत्वर्यमा
शन्न इन्द्रो बृहस्पतिः। शन्नो बिष्णुरुरुक्रमः।
नमो ब्रह्मणे । नमस्ते वायो। त्वमेव प्रत्यक्षं ब्रह्मासि।
त्वमेव प्रत्यक्षं ब्रह्म वदिष्यामि। ऋतं वदिष्यामि ।
सत्यं वदिष्यामि। तन्मामवतु। तद्वक्तारमवतु।
अवतु माम्। अवतु वक्तारम्।। ॐ शान्तिः शान्तिः शान्तिः।।

oṃ śanno mitraḥ śaṃ varuṇaḥ / śanno bhavatvaryamā
śanna indrobṛhaspatiḥ / śanno viṣṇururukramaḥ
namo brahmaṇe / namaste vāyo / tvameva pratyakṣaṃ brahmāsi
tvameva pratyakṣaṃ brahma vadiṣyāmi / ṛtaṃ vadiṣyāmi
satyaṃ vadiṣyāmi / tanmāmvatu / tadvaktāramavatu
avatu mām / avatu vaktāram / oṃ śāntiḥ śāntiḥ śāntiḥ

Sanskrit to English Word Meaning

śam - auspiciousness; *naḥ* - to us; *mitraḥ* - the sun deity; *śam* - auspiciousness; *varuṇaḥ* - the ocean deity; *śam* - auspiciousness; *naḥ* - to us; *bhavatu* - let (him) be; *aryamā* - lord of the manes; *śam* - auspiciousness; *naḥ* - to us; *indraḥ* - the ruler of *devatās*; *bṛhaspatiḥ* - the preceptor of *devatās*; *śam* - auspiciousness; *naḥ* - to us; *viṣṇuḥ* - the all pervasive sustainer of creation; *urukramaḥ* - the cosmic Lord; *namaḥ* - salutation; *brahmaṇe* - to the creator; *namaḥ* - salutation; *te* - to you; *vāyo* - O deity of wind; *tvam eva* - you indeed; *pratyakṣam* - perceptible; *brahma* - the truth; *asi* - are; *tvam eva* - you indeed; *pratyakṣam* - perceptible; *brahma* - the truth; *vadiṣyāmi* - I declare (understand); *ṛtam* - proper understanding; *vadiṣyāmi* - I declare (understand); *satyam* - truthfulness in speech; *vadiṣyāmi* - I declare (understand); *tat* - it; *mām* - me; *avatu* - may protect; *tat* - it; *vaktāram* - the teacher; *avatu* - may protect; *avatu* - may protect; *mām* - me; *avatu* - may protect; *vaktāram* - the teacher; *oṃ śāntiḥ śāntiḥ śāntiḥ* - *om* peace, peace, peace

Translation

May the sun deity give us auspiciousness. May the ocean deity give us auspiciousness. May the lord of manes give us auspiciousness. May the ruler of *devatās* and the preceptor of *devatās* give us auspiciousness. May the all pervasive sustainer of creation, Lord *Vāmana*, give us auspiciousness. Salutations to the creator. Salutations to you, O deity of wind! You indeed are the perceptible truth. I understand you to be the perceptible truth. I declare you to be the right understanding. I understand you to be the truthfulness in speech. May the truth protect me. May the truth protect the teacher. May the truth protect me. May the truth protect the teacher. *Om* peace, peace, peace.

Brief Explanation

This is the opening *mantra* of the *Taittirīya Upaniṣad* from the *Kṛṣṇa Yajur Veda*. The subject matter of the *Upaniṣads* is *Brahma-vidyā*, knowledge of the self. Self-knowledge reveals the essential nature of the self as being non-separate from the Lord. A seeker seeks blessings of various *devatās* for gaining this knowledge. The study of the *Upaniṣads* is not undertaken without the help of a teacher who can unfold *Brahma-vidyā*. In this prayer, one seeks protection for oneself and the teacher so that there may be no hindrance in the fulfillment of the pursuit. This prayer may be recited by the student before undertaking any study. (This prayer should be learned and recited using the three *svaras*, tones that are used in Vedic chanting.)

Bhojanāt Prāk

ब्रह्मार्पणं ब्रह्महविः ब्रह्माग्नौ ब्रह्मणाहुतम्।
ब्रह्मैव तेन गन्तव्यं ब्रह्मकर्मसमाधिना।।

brahmārpaṇāṃ brahmahaviḥ brahmāgnau brahmaṇā hutam
brahmaiva tena gantavyaṃ brahmakarmasamādhinā

Sanskrit to English Word Meaning

brahma - *Brahman*; *arpaṇām* - the means of offering; *brahma* - *brahman*; *haviḥ* - oblation; *brahmāgnau* - unto the fire that is *Brahman*; *brahmaṇā* - by *Brahman*; *hutam* - is offered; *brahma* - *Brahman*; *eva* - indeed; *tena* - by him; *gantavyam* - to be reached; *brahma-karma-samādhinā* - by the one who is abiding in *Brahman*

Translation

Any means of offering is *Brahman*, the oblation is *Brahman*, the fire in which the offering is made is *Brahman*, the one who offers is also *Brahman*. Indeed *Brahman* is gained by such a person who abides in *Brahman*.

Brief Explanation

This verse from the *Bhagavad Gītā* (Chapter 4, verse 24) is commonly chanted before meals. *Brahman* is the name for the Lord, the cause of the whole creation. Looking at the whole creation as an effect, *Brahman* is seen as the cause of everything. The effect does not exist separate from its cause. For example, a golden chain (effect) does not exist separate from gold (its cause). In fact, from the standpoint of its reality, the 'chain' is only a name given to a particular form of gold; what is, is only gold.

The first part of this verse shows *Brahman* as the cause or the basis of all that exists, and the effect as apparent differences that are only incidental. The verse refers to an offering made during a ritual. The person performing the ritual, the process of offering, the oblation and the fire are all *Brahman*. The differences of name and form that exist are only incidental. The one who recognises his or her identity with that undivided cause enjoys freedom and happiness.

The verse likens food that is eaten to an oblation poured into the fire during a ritual. The digestive fire is called *jāṭharāgni*, and in common speech, the metabolic process of degradation of carbohydrate is referred to as 'burning sugar'. In addition, by chanting this prayer before meals, the food that is eaten is offered to *Brahman*, the Lord.

Śayana Samaye

करचरणकृतं वाक्कायजं कर्मजं वा श्रवणनयनजं वा मानसं वाऽपराधम्।
विहितमविहितं वा सर्वमेतत्क्षमस्व जयजय करुणाब्धे श्रीमहादेव शम्भो ॥

karacaraṇakṛtaṃ vākkāyajaṃ karmajam vā
śravaṇanayanajaṃvā mānasaṃ vā'parādham
vihitamavihitaṃ vā sarvametatkṣamasva
jaya jaya karuṇābhde śrīmahādeva śambho

Sanskrit to English Word Meaning

kara-caraṇa-kṛtam - done by hands and feet; *vāk-kāyajaṃ* - born of the organ of speech and physical body; *karmajam* - born of performance of action; *vā* - or; *śravaṇa-nayanajaṃ* - born of ears and eyes; *vā* - or; *mānasam* - born of mind; *vā* - or; *aparādham* - omissions and commissions; *vihitam* - enjoined acts; *avihitaṃ* - prohibited acts; *vā* - or; *sarvam* - all; *etat* - these; *kṣamasva* - forgive; *jaya jaya* - may you be victorious; *karuṇābhḍe* - ocean of kindness; *śrīmahādeva* - O great Lord *Śiva*; *śambho* - O one who causes happiness, *Śambhu*

Translation

Lord, kindly forgive all the omissions and commissions born of my eyes, ears, mind and organ of speech, or done by my hands and feet, and the omissions and commissions in the performance of my duties, either enjoined or prohibited. Victory to you, O great Lord *Śiva*, the one who is the ocean of kindness, and the cause of happiness!

Brief Explanation

Before going to sleep, one ends the day with this prayer. One asks the Lord for forgiveness for inappropriate actions that one may have knowingly or unknowingly done during the day. These actions may be physical, verbal, or mental. Prayer itself is an action that has its own result in the form of *puṇya*, which neutralises the *pāpas* born of errors of omission and commission. Prayer is an appreciation of one's limitations, and a request for the blessings of the Lord for inner maturity and strength.

Śrī Rāmaḥ

रामाय रामभद्राय रामचन्द्राय वेधसे।
रघुनाथाय नाथाय सीतायाः पतये नमः॥

rāmāya rāmabhadrāya rāmacandrāya vedhase
raghunāthāya nāthāya sītāyāḥ pataye namaḥ

Sanskrit to English Word Meaning

rāmāya - unto Lord *Rāma*; *rāma-bhadrāya* - the auspicious *Rāma*; *rāma-candrāya* - *Rāma*, the shining light; *vedhase* - who is the creator; *raghu-nāthāya* - who is the Lord of *Raghu* clan; *nāthāya* - the Lord of all beings; *sītāyāḥ* - of *Sītā*; *pataye* - to the husband; *namaḥ* - salutation

Translation

Salutations unto Lord *Rāma*, who is auspiciousness, who is in the form of the shining light (consciousness present in all beings), who is the creator, who is the Lord of the *Raghu* clan, the Lord of all beings and the husband of *Sītā*.

Brief Explanation

The etymological meaning of the word '*Rāma*' is 'the one in whom the devotees revel'. As the Lord, *Rāma* also revels in all beings in the form of consciousness. Lord *Rāma* is the *avatāra* who exemplifies a life of *dharma*. He destroyed the *adharma* that was rampant in his time. An understanding of Lord *Rāma's* commitment to *dharma*, in the face of all adversities, helps one live up to one's life.

Śrī Kṛṣṇaḥ

वसुदेवसुतं देवं कंसचाणूरमर्दनम् ॥
देवकीपरमानन्दं कृष्णं वन्दे जगद्गुरुम् ॥

vasudevasutaṃ devaṃ kaṃsacāṇūramardanam
devakīparamānandaṃ kṛṣṇaṃ vande jagadgurum

Sanskrit to English Word Meaning

vasudevasutam - son of *Vasudeva*; *devam* - the Lord; *kaṃsa-cāṇūra-mardanam* - destroyer of *Kaṃsa* and *Cāṇūra* (demonic kings); *devakī-parama-ānandam* - the greatest joy of *Devakī* (*Kṛṣṇa's* mother); *kṛṣṇam* - Lord *Kṛṣṇa*; *vande* - I salute; *jagadgurum* - the teacher of the world

Translation

I salute *Kṛṣṇa*, the Lord, the teacher of the world, son of *Vasudeva*, destroyer of *Kaṃsa* and *Cāṇūra*, and the greatest joy of *Devakī*.

Brief Explanation

In this prayer one salutes Lord *Kṛṣṇa* in the form of *jagadguru*, universal teacher. The Lord is looked upon as a *jagadguru*, since the Lord's message in the *Bhagavad Gītā* is meant for humanity. Even though the Lord's essential nature is one of formlessness, Lord is described as above, for the purpose of visualisation and worship.

Śrī Hanumān

मनोजवं मारुततुल्यवेगं जितेन्द्रियं बुद्धिमतां वरिष्ठम्।
वातात्मजं वानरयूथमुख्यं श्रीरामदूतं शिरसा नमामि।।

manojavaṃ mārutatulyavegaṃ jitendriyaṃ buddhimatāṃ variṣṭham
vātātmajaṃ vānarayūthamukhyaṃ śrīrāmadūtaṃ śirasā namāmi

Sanskrit to English Word Meaning

manojavam - the speed of the mind; *māruta-tulya-vegam* - equal in speed to the wind; *jitendriyam* - one who has mastered his sense organs; *buddhimatām* - among the intelligent; *variṣṭham* - who is the best; *vātātmajam* - who is the son of the wind deity; *vānara-yūtha-mukhyam* - who is the chief of the army of the *vānara* tribe; *śrī-rāma-dūtam* - the envoy of *Rāma*; *śirasā* - by bowing my head; *namāmi* - I salute

Translation

Bowing my head, I salute *Hanumān*, who travels as fast as the mind and the wind, who has mastered his sense organs, who is the best among the intelligent, who is the son of the deity of wind, who is the commander-in-chief of the army of the *vānara* tribe, and who is the envoy of *Śrī Rāma*.

Brief Explanation

Lord *Hanumān* is an embodiment of devotion. His devotion to Lord *Rāma* allowed him to accomplish seemingly impossible tasks. Lord *Hanumān* is prayed to for strength and devotion. Traditionally, just as prayers and devotional songs begin with a salutation to Lord *Gaṇeśa*, they usually end with a prayer or a song in praise of Lord *Hanumān*.

Guru Vandanam

श्रुतिस्मृतिपुराणानाम् आलयं करुणालयम् ।
नमामि भगवत्पादं शङ्करं लोकशङ्करम् ।।१।।

śrutismṛtipurāṇānām ālayaṃ karuṇālayam
namāmi bhagavatpādaṃ śaṅkaraṃ lokaśaṅkaraṃ (1)

śruti-smṛti-purāṇānām - of the *śruti* (*Vedas*), *smṛti* (*Gītā* etc.) and *purāṇas*; *ālayam* - the abode; *karuṇālayam* - the repository of compassion; *namāmi* - I salute; *bhagavat-pādam* - one who is revered; *śaṅkaram* - *Ādi Śaṅkarācārya*; *loka-śaṅkaram* - the one who gives happiness to the world

I salute *Ādi Śaṅkarācārya*, the abode of the *śruti* (*Vedas*), *smṛti* (*Gītā* etc.) and *purāṇas*, the repository of compassion, the one who gives happiness to the world and one who is revered.

शङ्करं शङ्कराचार्यं केशवं बादरायणम् ।
सूत्रभाष्यकृतौ वन्दे भगवन्तौ पुनः पुनः ।।२।।

śaṅkaraṃ śaṅkarācāryaṃ keśavaṃ bādarāyaṇam
sūtrabhāṣyakṛtau vande bhagavantau punaḥ punaḥ (2)

śaṅkaram - Lord *Śiva*; *śaṅkarācāryam* - the great teacher *Ādi Śaṅkarācārya*; *keśavam* - Lord *Viṣṇu*; *bādarāyaṇam* - *Śrī Vyāsa*; *sūtra-bhāṣya-kṛtau* - those who wrote the aphorisms (*Brahma-sūtras*) and the commentaries (*Bhāṣyas*); *vande* - I salute; *bhagavantau* - the venerable ones; *punaḥ punaḥ* - again and again

I salute, again and again, the great teacher *Ādi Śaṅkarācārya*, who is Lord *Śiva* and *Bādarāyaṇa*, who is Lord *Viṣṇu*, the venerable ones who wrote the *Bhaṣyas* and the *Brahma-sūtras* respectively.

ईश्वरो गुरुरात्मेति मूर्त्तिभेदविभागिने ।
व्योमवद्व्याप्तदेहाय दक्षिणामूर्त्तये नमः ।।३।।

īśvaro gururātmeti mūrttibheda vibhāgine
vyomavadvyāptadehāya daksṇāmūrttaye namaḥ (3)

īśvaraḥ - the Lord; *guruḥ* - the teacher; *ātmā* - the self; *iti* - thus; *mūrtti-bheda-vibhāgine* - the one who appears (as though) divided; *vyomavat* - like space; *vyāpta-dehāya* - to one who is all pervasive; *dakṣiṇāmūrtaye* - to Lord *Dakṣiṇāmūrti*; *namaḥ* - salutation

Salutation to Lord *Dakṣiṇāmūrti*, who is all pervasive like space, but who appears (as though) divided as the Lord, the teacher and the self.

गुकारस्त्वन्धकारो वै रुकारस्तन्निवर्त्तकः।
अन्धकारनिरोधित्वाद् गुरुरित्यभिधीयते॥ ४॥

gukārastvandhakāro vai rukārastannivarttakaḥ
andhakāranirodhitvād gururityabhidhīyate (4)

gukāraḥ - the syllable '*gu*'; *tu* - indeed; *andhakāraḥ* - (stands for) darkness (of ignorance); *vai* - indeed; *rukāraḥ* - the syllable '*ru*'; *tad-nivarttakaḥ* - its remover; *andhakāra-nirodhitvāt* - because he destroys the darkness (of ignorance); *guruḥ* - a *guru*; *iti* - thus; *abhidhīyate* - is so called

The syllable '*gu*' stands for darkness (of ignorance) and '*ru*' represents its remover. A *guru* is so called because he removes the darkness (of ignorance).

सदाशिवसमारम्भां शङ्कराचार्यमध्यमाम्।
अस्मदाचार्यपर्यन्तां वन्दे गुरुपरम्पराम् ॥ ५॥

sadāśivasamārambhāṃ śaṅkarācāryamadhyamām
asmadācāryaparyantāṃ vande guruparamparām (5)

sadāśiva-samārambhām - beginning with the ever auspicious Lord *Śiva*; *śaṅkarācārya-madhyamām* - *Ādi Śaṅkarācārya* in the middle; *asmad-ācāryaparyantām*- up to our teacher; *vande* - I salute; *guru-paramparām* - the lineage of teachers

I salute the lineage of teachers, beginning with the ever auspicious Lord *Śiva*, (linked by) *Ādi Śaṅkarācārya* in the middle and extending up to my own teacher.

Dakṣiṇāmūrti Dhyānaślokas

मौनव्याख्याप्रकटितपरब्रह्मतत्वं युवानं
वर्षिष्ठान्तेवसदृषिगणैरावृतं ब्रह्मनिष्ठैः।
आचार्येन्द्रं करकलित चिन्मुद्रमानन्दरूपं
स्वात्मारामं मुदितवदनं दक्षिणामूर्तिमीडे॥१॥

maunavyākhyāprakaṭitaparabrahmatatvaṃ yuvānaṃ
varṣiṣṭhāntevasadṛṣigaṇairāvṛtaṃ brahmaniṣṭhaiḥ
ācāryendraṃ karakalitacinmudramānandarūpam
svātmārāmaṃ muditavadanaṃ dakṣiṇāmūrtimīḍe (1)

mauna-vyākhyā-prakaṭita-parabrahma-tatvam - the one, who expounded the truth of nondual *Brahman* through silence; *yuvānam* - the ageless; *varṣiṣṭha-antevasad-ṛṣigaṇaiḥ* - by the group of sages sitting near and who are aged; *āvṛtam* - surrounded; *brahma-niṣṭhaiḥ* - by those who ever abide in *Brahman*; *ācāryendram* - who is the best among the teachers; *karakalita-cinmudram* - one whose hand is held in the gesture of *cinmudrā*; *ānandarūpam* - one who is the embodiment of joy; *svātmārāmam* - one who revels in himself; *muditavadanam* - one who has a smiling countenance; *dakṣiṇāmūrtim* - Lord *Dakṣiṇāmūrtim*; *īḍe* - I praise

I praise Lord *Dakṣiṇāmūrti*, the ageless one, who expounded the truth of nondual *Brahman* through silence, who is surrounded by aged disciples, who ever abide in *Brahman*, who is the best among teachers, whose hand is held in the gesture of *cinmudrā*, who is the embodiment of joy, who revels in himself and who has a smiling countenance.

वटविटपिसमिपे भूमिभागेनिषण्णं
सकलमुनिजनानां ज्ञानदातारमारात्।
त्रिभुवनगुरुमीशं दक्षिणामूर्तिदेवं
जननमरणदुःखच्छेददक्षं नमामि॥२ ॥

vaṭaviṭapisamīpe bhūmibhāge niṣaṇṇam
sakalamunijanānāṃ jñānadātārmārāt
tribhuvanagurumīśaṃ dakṣiṇāmūrtidevaṃ
jananamaraṇaduḥkhacchedadakṣaṃ namāmi (2)

vaṭa-viṭapi-samīpe - near the banyan tree; *bhūmi-bhāge* - on the ground; *niṣaṇṇam* - seated; *sakala-muni-janānāṃ* - of all the sages; *jñāna-dātārm* - the giver of knowledge; *ārāt* - near; *tribhuvanagurum* - the teacher of the three worlds; *īśaṃ* - the Lord; *dakṣiṇāmūrti-devaṃ* - the deity *Dakṣiṇāmūrti*; *janana-maraṇa-duḥkhaccheda-dakṣaṃ* - the one who is adept at destroying the miseries of birth and death; *namāmi* - I salute

I salute Lord *Dakṣiṇāmūrti*, the teacher of the three worlds, who is adept at destroying the miseries of birth and death, who, seated on the ground under the banyan tree, bestows knowledge to all the sages near him.

चित्रं वटतरोर्मूले वृद्धाश्शिष्या गुरुर्युवा ।
गुरोस्तु मौनं व्याख्यानं शिष्यास्तु छिन्नसंशयाः ॥ ३ ॥
citraṃ vaṭatarormūle vṛddhāśśiṣyā gururyuvā
gurostu maunaṃ vyākhyānaṃ śiṣyāstu chinnasaṃśayāḥ (3)

citram - it is (indeed) a wonder; *vaṭa-taroḥ* - of a banyan tree; *mūle* - beneath; *vṛddhāḥ* - the aged; *śiṣyāḥ* - disciples; *guruḥ* - the teacher; *yuvā* - young; *guroḥ* - of the *guru*; *tu* - indeed; *maunam* - silence; *vyākhyānam* - the exposition; *śiṣyāḥ* - the disciples; *tu* - whereas; *chinna-saṃśayāḥ* - remain with their doubts dispelled

It is (indeed) a wonder! Under the banyan tree were the aged disciples around the ever-young *guru*! The exposition of the *guru* was silence and the doubts of the disciples were dispelled.

निधये सर्वविद्यानां भिषजे भवरोगिणाम् ।
गुरवे सर्वलोकानां दक्षिणामूर्तये नमः ॥ ४ ॥

nidhaye sarvavidyānāṃ bhiṣaje bhavaroginạ̄m
gurave sarvalokānāṃ dakṣṇāmūrtaye namaḥ (4)

nidhaye - to the abode; *sarva-vidyānāṃ* - of all learning; *bhiṣaje* - the healer; *bhavaroginạ̄m* - of the disease of all sorrows; *gurave* - to the teacher; *sarva-lokānām* - of all the worlds; *dakṣṇāmūrtaye* - unto Lord *Dakṣṇāmūrti*; *namaḥ* - salutations

Salutation to Lord *Dakṣṇāmūrti*, who is the abode of all learning, who is the remover of all sorrows born of limitations and who is the teacher of all the worlds.

ॐ नमः प्रणवार्थाय शुद्धज्ञानैकमूर्तये ।
निर्मलाय प्रशान्ताय दक्षिणामूर्तये नमः ॥ ५ ॥
oṃ namaḥ praṇavārthāya śuddhajñānaikamūrtaye

nirmalāya praśāntāya dakṣiṇāmūrtaye namaḥ (5)

om - the Lord; *namaḥ* - salutation; *praṇavārthāya* - to the essence of *om*; *śuddha-jñānaika-mūrtaye* - who is the very embodiment of knowledge; *nirmalāya* - who is ever pure; *praśāntāya* - tranquil; *dakṣiṇāmūrtaye* - to Lord *Dakṣiṇāmūrti*; *namaḥ* - salutation

Salutation to Lord *Dakṣiṇāmūrti*, who is the essence of *Om*, who is the very embodiment of pure knowledge and who is ever pure and tranquil.

Selections from *Gītā Dhyānam*

First Verse:

ॐ पार्थाय प्रतिबोधितां भगवता नारायणेन स्वयं
व्यासेन ग्रथितां पुराणमुनिना मध्येमहाभारतम।
अद्वैतामृतवर्षिणीं भगवतीम् अष्टादशाध्यायिनीं
अम्ब त्वामनूसन्दधामि भगवद्गीते भवद्वेषिणीम ।।१।।

oṃ pārthāya pratibodhitāṃ bhagavatā nārāyaṇena svayaṃ
vyāsena grathitāṃ purāṇamuninā madhyemahābhārtam
advaitāmṛtavarṣiṇīṃ bhagavatīm aṣṭādaśādhyāyinīm
amba tvāmanusandadhāmi bhagavadgīte bhavadveṣiṇīm (1)

om - *om*; *pārthāya* - for the sake of *Arjuna*, the son of *Pṛthā* (*Kuntī*); *pratibodhitām* - taught; *bhagavatā* - by Lord; *nārāyaṇena* - by *Nārāyaṇa*; *svayam* - himself; *vyāsena* - by *Vyāsa*; *grathitām* - faithfully collected and reported; *purāṇa-muninā* - by the ancient sage; *madhye-mahābhārtam* - in the middle of the *Mahābhārta*; *advaita-amṛta-varṣiṇīm* - showering the nectar of nonduality; *bhagavatīm* - the Goddess; *aṣṭādaśa-adhyāyinīm* - of eighteen chapters; *amba* - O Mother; *tvām* - you; *anusandadhāmi* - I repeatedly invoke; *bhagavadgīte* - O *Bhagavad Gītā*; *bhava-dveṣiṇīm* - destroyer of the life of becoming

Om O Goddess Mother, O *Bhagavad Gītā*, taught by Lord *Nārāyaṇa* himself for the sake of *Arjuna*, the son of *Pṛthā* (*Kuntī*), faithfully collected and reported by the ancient Sage *Vyāsa*, (and placed) in the middle of *Mahābhārta*, comprised of eighteen chapters, showering the nectar of nonduality, the destroyer of the life of becoming, I invoke you again and again.

Last verse :

यं ब्रह्मा वरुणेन्द्ररुद्रमरुतः स्तुन्वन्ति दिव्यैस्स्तवैः
वेदैस्साङ्गपदक्रमोपनिषदैः गायन्ति यं सामगाः ।
ध्यानावस्थिततद्गतेन मनसा पश्यन्ति यं योगिनः

यस्यान्तं न विदुस्सुरासुरगणा देवाय तस्मै नमः ।। २ ।।

yaṃ brahmā varuṇendrarudramarutaḥ stunvanti divyaisstavaḥ
vedaissāṅgapadakramopaniṣadaiḥ gāyanti yaṃ sāmagāḥ
dhyānāvasthitatadgatena manasā paśyanti yaṃ yoginaḥ
yasyāntaṃ na vidussurāsuragaṇā devāya tasmai namaḥ (2)

yam - whom; *brahmā* - *Brahmā*; *varuṇa-indra-rudra-marutaḥ* - *Varuṇa*, *Indra*, *Rudra* and *Marut*; *stunvanti* - sing in praise; *divyaḥ-stavaḥ*- with divine hymns; *vedaiḥ* - by the *Vedas*; *sa-aṅga-pada-krama-upaniṣadaiḥ* - with a full complement of the limbs (of singing) in the order of the *pada* and *krama* and *Upaniṣads*; *gāyanti* - sing in praise; *yam* - whom; *sāmagāḥ* - the singers of the *Sāma-Veda*; *dhyānāvasthita-tad-gatena manasā* - with a mind resolved in him in a state of meditation; *paśyanti* - see clearly; *yam* - whom; *yoginaḥ* - contemplative people; *yasya* - whose; *antam* - nature; *na viduḥ* - do not know; *sura-asura-gaṇāḥ* - the celestials and the demons; *devāya* - to the Lord; *tasmai* - unto him; *namaḥ* - my salutation

The Lord about whom *Brahmā*, *Varuṇa*, *Indra*, *Rudra* and *Marut* sing divine hymns of praise, the one whom the singers of the *Sāma-Veda* praise by singing with a full complement of the limbs (of singing), in the order of the *pada* and *krama* and *Upaniṣads*, the one who is seen clearly by contemplative people with minds resolved in him in a state of meditation, whose nature the celestials and the demons do not know, unto that Lord my salutations.

Selections from *Bhagavad Gītā*, Ch.15

(Verses chanted before eating food)

यदादित्यगतं तेजः जगद्भासयतेऽखिलम्।
यच्चन्द्रमसि यच्चाग्नौ तत्तेजो विद्धि मामकम्।।१२।।

yadādityagataṃ tejaḥ jagadbhāsayate'khilam
yaccandramasi yaccāgnau tattejo viddhi māmakam (12)

yat - which; *āditya-gatam* - in the sun; *tejaḥ* - the light; *jagat* - universe; *bhāsayate* - illumines; *akhilam* - the entire; *yat* - which; *candramasi* - (the light) in the moon; *yat* - which; *ca* - and; *agnau* - (the light) in the fire; *tat* - that; *tejaḥ* - light; *viddhi* - you understand; *māmakam* - to be mine

The light in the sun which illumines the entire universe, (the light) in the moon and (the light) in the fire - may you understand that light to be mine.

गामाविश्य च भूतानि धारयाम्यहमोजसा।
पुष्णामि चौषधीस्सर्वाः सोमोभूत्वा रसात्मकः।।१३।।

gāmāviśya ca bhūtāni dhārayāmyahamojasā
puṣṇāmi cauṣadhīssarvāḥ somobhūtvā rasātmakaḥ (13)

gām - the earth; *āviśya* - having entered; *ca* - and; *bhūtāni* - all beings; *dhārayāmi* - sustain; *aham* - I; *ojasā* - with my energy; *puṣṇāmi* - I nourish; *ca* - and; *oṣadhī* - plants; *sarvāḥ* - all; *somaḥ* - the moonlight; *bhūtvā* - having become; *rasātmakaḥ* - which is full of nourishment

Having entered the earth, I sustain all beings with my energy. Having become the moonlight which is full of nourishment, I nourish all plants.

अहं वैश्वानरो भूत्वा प्राणिनां देहमाश्रितः।
प्राणापानसमायुक्तः पचाम्यन्नं चतुर्विधम्।। १४।।

ahaṃ vaiśvānaro bhūtvā prāṇināṃ dehamāśritaḥ
prāṇāpānasamāyuktaḥ pacāmyannaṃ caturvidham (14)

aham - I; *vaiśvānaraḥ* - the digestive fire; *bhūtvā* - having become; *prāṇināṃ* - of living beings; *deham* - the body; *āśritaḥ* - residing in; *prāṇa-apāna-samāyuktaḥ* - and being supported by the ingoing and outgoing breath; *pacāmi* - digest; *annam* - food; *caturvidham* - the fourfold

Residing in the body of living beings as the digestive fire and being supported by the vital air, I digest the fourfold food.

सर्वस्य चाहं हृदि सन्निविष्टः
मत्तस्स्मृतिर्ज्ञानमपोहनं च।
वेदैश्च सर्वैरहमेव वेद्यः
वेदान्तकृद्वेदविदेव चाहम्।।१५।।

sarvasya cāhaṃ hṛdi sanniviṣṭaḥ
mattassmṛtirjñānamapohanaṃ ca
vedaiśca sarvairahameva vedyaḥ
vedāntakṛdvedavideva cāham (15)

sarvasya - of all; *ca* - and; *ahaṃ* - I; *hṛdi* - in the heart; *sanniviṣṭaḥ* - am seated; *mattaḥ* - are from me; *smṛtiḥ* - memory; *jñānam* - knowledge; *apohanaṃ* - forgetfulness; *ca* - and; *vedaiḥ* - by the *Vedas*; *ca* - and; *sarvaiḥ* - through all; *aham* - I; *eva* - alone; *vedyaḥ* - am to be known; *vedāntakṛt* - am the giver of *Vedānta*; *vedavit* - knower of the *Vedas*; *eva* - alone; *ca* - and; *aham* - I

I am seated in the hearts of all beings. Memory, knowledge and forgetfulness are from me alone. Through all the *Vedas* I alone am to be known. I am the giver of *Vedānta*, as well as the knower of the *Vedas*.

द्वाविमौ पुरुषौ लोके क्षरश्चाक्षर एव च ।
क्षरस्सर्वाणिभूतानि कूटस्थोऽक्षर उच्यते।।१६।।

dvavimau pururṣau loke kṣaraścākṣara eva ca
kṣarassarvāṇibhūtānikūṭastho'kṣara ucyate (16)

dvau - two; *imau* - these; *pururṣau* - entities; *loke* - in the world; *kṣaraḥ* - the perishable; *ca* - and; *akṣaraḥ* - the imperishable; *eva ca* - and; *kṣaraḥ* - the perishable; *sarvāṇi* - all; *bhūtāni* - beings; *kūṭasthaḥ* - the immutable (*māyā*); *akṣaraḥ* - the imperishable; *ucyate* - is said to be

These are the two entities in the world - the perishable and the imperishable. The perishable is in the form of all beings and the imperishable is said to be *māyā*.

उत्तमः पुरुषस्त्वन्यः परमात्मेत्युदाहृतः।
यो लोकत्रयमाविश्य बिभर्त्यव्यय ईश्वरः।।१७।।

uttamaḥ puruṣastvanyaḥ paramātmetyudāhṛtaḥ
yo lokatrayamāviśya bibhartyavyaya īśvaraḥ (17)

uttamaḥ - (is) the ultimate (truth); *puruṣaḥ* - being; *tu* - indeed; *anyaḥ* - different (from these); *paramātmā* - the ultimate truth; *iti* - thus; *udāhṛtaḥ* - said to be; *yaḥ* - who; *loka-trayam* - the three worlds; *āviśya* - having pervaded; *bibharti* - sustains; *avyayaḥ* - it is the imperishable; *īśvaraḥ* - the Lord

Paramātmā (the ultimate truth) is indeed distinct from these two. It pervades and sustains the three worlds. It is the imperishable Lord.

यस्मात्यक्षरमतीतोऽहम् अक्षरादपिचोत्तमः।
अतोऽस्मि लोके वेदे च प्रथितः पुरुषोत्तमः॥ १८॥

yasmātyakṣaramatīto'ham akṣrādapicottamaḥ
ato'smi loke vede ca prathitaḥ puruṣottamaḥ (18)

yasmāt - since; *kṣaram* - perishable; *atītaḥ* - am beyond; *aham* - I; *akṣarāt* - the imperishable; *api* - also; *ca* - and; *uttamaḥ* - more than; *ataḥ* - therefore; *asmi* - I am; *loke* - in the world; *vede* - in the *Vedas*; *ca* - and; *prathitaḥ* - well known; *puruṣottamaḥ* - as *puruṣottama*

Since I am beyond the perishable and more than the imperishable, I am well known in the world and in the *Vedas* as *puruṣottama.*

यो मामेवमसम्मूढः जानाति पुरुषोत्तमम्।
स सर्वविद्भजति मां सर्वभावेन भारत॥१९॥

yo māmevamasammūḍhaḥ jānāti puruṣottamam
sa sarvavidbhajati māṃ sarvabhāvena bhārata (19)

yaḥ - who; *mām* - me; *evam* - thus; *asammūḍhaḥ* - being free from delusion; *jānāti* - knows; *puruṣottamam* - *puruṣottama*; *saḥ* - he; *sarvavit* - knower of everything; *bhajati* - worships; *mām* - me; *sarvabhāvena* - wholeheartedly; *bhārata* - O *Arjuna*

Being free from delusion, he who knows me thus as *puruṣottama*, is the knower of everything and worships me wholeheartedly, O *Arjuna.*

इति गुह्यतमं शास्त्रम् इदमुक्तं मयानघ ।
एतद् बुद्ध्वा बुद्धिमान्स्यात् कृतकृत्यश्च भारत॥२०॥

iti guhyatamam śāstraṃ idamuktaṃ mayānagha
etad buddhvā buddhimān syāt kṛtakṛtyaśca bhārata (20)

iti - thus; *guhya-tamam* - most secret; *śāstram* - teaching; *idam* - this; *uktam* - has been imparted; *mayā* - by me; *anagha* - O *Arjuna*; *etat* - this; *buddhvā* - having known; *buddhimān* - wise; *syāt* - one becomes; *kṛtakṛtyaḥ* - fulfilled; *ca* - and; *bhārata* - O *Arjuna*

O *Arjuna*! Thus, this most secret teaching has been imparted by me. Having known this, one becomes wise and fulfilled.

ॐ तत्सत् इति श्रीमद्भगवद्गीतासु उपनिषत्सु ब्रह्मविद्यायां योगशास्त्रे
श्रीकृष्णार्जुनसंवादे पुरुषोत्तमयोगो नाम पञ्चदशोऽध्यायः ॥

oṃ tat sat iti śrīmadbhagavadgītāsu upaniṣatsu brahmavidyāyāṃ yogaśāstre
śrīkṛṣṇārjunasaṃvāde puruṣottamayogo nāma pañcadaśo'dhyāyaḥ

oṃ tat sat - with the utterance of the words '*om*', '*tat*' and '*sat*'; *iti* - thus; *śrīmadbhagavadgītāsu* - in *Śrīmad Bhagavad Gītā*; *upaniṣatsu* - which is an *Upaniṣad*; *brahmavidyāyām* - dealing with knowledge of *Brahman*; *yogaśāyogaśāstre* - and dealing with *yoga*; *śrī kṛṣṇārjuna-saṃvāde* - in the dialogue between *Śrī Kṛṣṇa* and *Arjuna*; *puruṣottama-yogaḥ nāma* - titled *Puruṣottama-yoga*; *pañcadaśaḥ adhyāyaḥ* - the fifteenth chapter (ends)

With the utterance of the words '*om*', '*tat*' and '*sat*', thus ends the fifteenth chapter called *Puruṣottama-yoga*, (the Chapter on the Supreme Lord) in the *Bhagavad Gītā* which is the essence of the *Upaniṣads*, whose subject matter is both the knowledge of *Brahman* and *yoga*, in the dialogue between *Śrī Kṛṣṇa* and *Arjuna*.

सर्वधर्मान्परित्यज्य मामेकं शरणं व्रज।
अहं त्वा सर्वपापेभ्यः मोक्षयिष्यामि मा शुचः ॥

sarvadharmān parityajya māmekaṃ śaraṇaṃvraja
ahaṃ tvā sarvapāpebhyaḥ mokṣayiṣyāmi mā śucaḥ

sarva-dharmān - all actions; *parityajya* - giving up; *mām* - in me; *ekam* - alone; *śaraṇam* - refuge; *vraja* - take; *aham* - I; *tvā* - you; *sarvapāpebhyaḥ* - from all *pāpas*; *mokṣayiṣyāmi* - will liberate; *mā* - (do) not; *śucaḥ* - grieve

Giving up all actions, take refuge in me alone. I will liberate you from all *pāpas*; do not grieve.

Part 7

Śrī Śiva Pañcākṣara Stotram

नागेन्द्रहाराय त्रिलोचनाय
भस्माङ्गरागाय महेश्वराय ।
नित्याय शुद्धाय दिगम्बराय
तस्मै नकाराय नमश्शिवाय ॥१॥

nāgendrahārāya trilocanāya
bhasmāṅgarāgāya maheśvarāya
nityāya śuddhāya digambarāya
tasmai nakārāya namaśśivāyā (1)

nāgendra-hārāya - to the one who wears the serpent king as a garland; *trilocanāya* - who has three eyes; *bhasmāṅga-rāgāya* - who has ashes smeared all over his body; *maheśvarāya* - who is the Lord of the deities; *nityāya* - who is timeless; *śuddhāya* - who is pure; *digambarāya* - whose clothing is the sky; *tasmai* - unto him; *nakārāya* - who is in the form of the syllable '*na*'; *namaḥ* - salutation; *śivāyā* - to Lord *Śiva*

My salutation to Lord *Śiva*, who is in the form of the syllable '*na*', who wears the serpent king as a garland, who has three eyes, who has ashes smeared all over his body, who is the supreme Lord, who is eternal and pure and whose clothing is the sky.

मन्दाकिनीसलिलचन्दनचर्चिताय
नन्दीश्वरप्रमथनाथमहेश्वराय ।
मन्दारपुष्पबहुपुष्पसुपूजिताय
तस्मै मकाराय नमश्शिवाय ॥२॥

mandākinīsalilacandanacarcitāya
nandīśvarapramathanāthamaheśvarāya
mandārapuṣpabahupuṣpasupūjitāya
tasmai makārāya namaśśivāya (2)

mandākinī-salila-candana-carcitāya - to the one who is anointed with the waters of the

Mandākinī (Gaṅgā) and the sandalpaste; *nandīśvara-pramatha-nātha-maheśvarāya* - who is the supreme Lord of *Nandi* and the other leaders of the troop of attendants; *mandārapuṣpa bahupuṣpa-supūjitāya* - who is elaborately worshipped with many flowers including *mandāra* flower; *tasmai* - to him; *makārāya* - who is in the form of the syllable '*ma*'; *namaḥ* - salutation; *śivāya* - to Lord *Śiva*

My salutation to Lord *Śiva* who is in the form of the syllable '*ma*', who is bathed with waters of *Gaṅgā* and sandalpaste, who is the supreme Lord of *Nandi* and the other leaders of the troop of attendants in *Kailāsa* and who is elaborately worshipped with *mandāra* and many other flowers.

शिवाय गौरीवदनाब्जवृन्द-
सूर्याय दक्षाध्वरनाशकाय।
श्रीनीलकण्ठाय वृषध्वजाय
तस्मै शिकाराय नमश्शिवाय ।। ३।।

śivāya gaurīvadanābjavṛnda-
sūryāya dakṣādhvaranāśakāya
śrīnīlakaṇṭhāya vṛṣadhvajāya
tasmai śikārāya namaśśivāya (3)

śivāya - to Lord *Śiva*; *gaurī-vadanābja-vṛnda-sūryāya* - who is like the sun to cluster of lotuses which is likened to *Pārvatī*'s face; *dakṣādhvara-nāśakāya* - who destroyed *Dakṣa*'s sacrifice; *śrī-nīlakaṇṭhāya* - the aupicious one who has a blue neck; *vṛṣa-dhvajāya* - who has the bull inscription on his banner; *tasmai* - to him; *śikārāya* - who is in the form of the syllable '*śi*'; *namaḥ* - salutation; *śivāya* - to Lord *Śiva*

My salutation to Lord *Śiva* the blessed one who has a blue neck, who is in the form of the syllable '*śi*', who is the sun to the cluster of lotuses that is likened to *Pārvatī*'s face, who destroyed *Dakṣa*'s sacrifice and who has the bull inscription on his banner.

वसिष्ठकुम्भोद्भवगौतमार्य-
मुनीन्द्रदेवार्चितशेखराय ।
चन्द्रार्कवैश्वानरलोचनाय
तस्मै वकाराय नमश्शिवाय ।।४।।

vasiṣṭhakumbhodbhavagautamārya-
munīndradevārcitaśekharāya
candrārkavaiśvānaralocanāya
tasmai vakārāya namaśśivāya (4)

vasiṣṭha-kumbhodbhava-gautamārya-munīndra-devārcita-śekharāya - to the Lord whose head is adored by great sages including *Vasiṣṭha*, *Agastya* and *Gautama* as well as by the gods; *candrārka-vaiśvānara-locanāya* - who has the sun, the moon and fire as his three eyes; *tasmai* -

to him; *vakārāya* - who is in the form of the syllable '*va*'; *namaḥ* - salutation; *śivāya* - to Lord *Śiva*

My salutation to Lord *Śiva* who is in the form of the syllable '*va*', who is adored by the great sages including *Vasiṣṭha, Agastya, Gautama* as well as the gods and whose eyes are the sun, moon and fire.

यक्षस्वरूपाय जटाधराय
पिनाकहस्ताय सनातनाय ।
दिव्याय देवाय दिगम्बराय
तस्मै यकाराय नमश्शिवाय ॥ ५॥

yakṣasvarūpāya jaṭādharāya
pinākahastāya sanātanāya
divyāya devāya digambarāya
tasmai yakārāya namaśśivāya (5)

yakṣa-svarūpāya - to the one who is in the form of *yakṣa* (a celestial being); *jaṭādharāya* - who has a braid of matted locks; *pinākahastāya* - who holds the *pināka* bow in his arms; *sanātanāya* - who is the most ancient being; *divyāya-devāya* - who is the shining god; *digambarāya* - whose clothes are the four directions; *tasmai* - to him; *yakārāya* - who is in the form of the syllable '*ya*'; *namaḥ* - salutation; *śivāya* - to Lord *Śiva*

My salutation to Lord *Śiva*, who is in the form of the syllable '*ya*', who appeared once as a *yakṣa*, who has a braid of matted locks, who holds the *pināka* bow in his arm and who is the most ancient, the shining Lord whose clothes are the four directions.

पञ्चाक्षरमिदं पुण्यं यः पठेच्छिवसन्निधौ।
शिवलोकमवाप्नोति शिवेन सह मोदते ॥

pañcākṣaramidaṃ puṇyaṃ yaḥ paṭhecchivasannidhau
śivalokamavāpnoti śivena saha modate

pañcākṣaram - the five syllabled hymn; *idam* - this; *puṇyam* - meritorious; *yaḥ* - (one) who; *paṭhet*- recites; *śiva-sannidhau*- in the shrine of Lord *Śiva*; *śivalokam*- the abode of *Śiva*; *avāpnoti* - he gains; *śivena saha* - along with Lord *Śiva*; *modate* - rejoices

He, who recites this meritorious five-syllabled hymn in the shrine of Lord *Śiva* gains the abode of *Śiva* and rejoices with the Lord.

Gaṅgā Stotram

देवि सुरेश्वरि भगवति गङ्गेó
त्रिभुवनतारिणि तरलतरङ्गे ।
शङ्करमौलिविहारिणि विमलेô
मम मतिरास्तां तवपदकमले ॥१॥

devi sureśvari bhagavati gaṅge
tribhuvanatāriṇi taralataraṅge
śaṅkaramaulivihāriaṇi vimale
mama mati rāstāṃ tavapadakamale (1)

devi - O Goddess!; *sureśvari* - who is the ruler of all the *devatās*; *bhagavati* - who is endowed with all the glories; *gaṅge* - O *Gaṅgā*!; *tribhuvana-tāriṇi* - who takes one beyond the three worlds; *tarala-taraṅge* - who has pure white waves; *śaṅkara-mauli-vihāriaṇi* - who adorns the matted hair of Lord *Śiva*; *vimale* - who is pure; *mama* - my; *matiḥ* - mind; *āstām*- let it abide; *tava* - your; *pada-kamale* - at the lotus feet

O Goddess *Gaṅgā*, who is the ruler of all the *devatās*, who is endowed with all the glories, who is pure, who takes one beyond the three worlds, who has pure white waves and who adorns the matted hair of Lord *Śiva*, may my mind rest at your lotus feet.

भागीरथि सुखदायिनि मातः
तव जलमहिमा निगमे ख्यातः।
नाहं जाने तव महिमानं
पाहि कृपामयि मामज्ञानम्॥ २॥

bhāgīrathi sukhadāyini mātaḥ
tava jalamahimā nigame khyātaḥ
nāhaṃ jāne tava mahimānaṃ
pāhi kṛpāmayi māmajñānam (2)

bhāgīrathi - O *Bhāgīrathi*!; *sukhadāyini* - who gives happiness to all beings; *mātaḥ* - O Mother!; *tava* - your; *jala-mahimā* - the glory of waters; *nigame* - in the scriptures; *khyātaḥ* - described; *na* - not; *aham* - I; *jāne* - know; *tava* - your; *mahimānam* - glory; *pāhi* - protect; *kṛpā-mayi* - O compassionate one!; *mām* - me; *ajñānam* - the ignorant

O Mother *Bhāgīrathi*! the one who gives happiness to all, the glory of your waters has been described in the scriptures. But I do not know (all your) glory. O compassionate one! please protect me, the ignorant.

हरिपदपाद्यतरङ्गिणि गङ्गे
हिमविधुमुक्ताधवलतरङ्गे ।
दूरीकुरु मम दुष्कृतिभारं
कुरु कृपया भवसागरपारम् ॥ ३ ॥

haripadapādyataraṅgiṇi gaṅge
himavidhumuktādhavalataraṅge
dūrīkuru mama duṣkṛtibhāraṃ
kuru kṛpayā bhavasāgarapāram (3)

hari-pada-pādya-taraṅgiṇi - the one who has come down from the feet of Lord *Viṣṇu*; *gaṅge* - O *Gaṅgā*!; *hima-vidhu-muktā-dhavala-taraṅge* - whose rapids are as white as snow, moon and pearl; *dūrīkuru* - may you remove; *mama* - my; *duṣkṛti-bhāraṃ* - the load of misdeeds; *kuru* - may you do; *kṛpayā* - with compassion; *bhava-sāgara-pāram* - (my) crossing of the ocean of sorrow

O *Gaṅgā*! the one who has come down from the feet of Lord *Viṣṇu* and whose rapids are as white as snow, as the moon and as a pearl, may you remove the load of my misdeeds and kindly help me cross the ocean of sorrow.

तवजलममलं येन निपीतं
परमपदं खलु तेन गृहीतम्।
मातर्गङ्गे त्वयि यो भक्तः
किल तं द्रष्टुं न यमश्शक्तः ॥ ४ ॥

tava jalamamalaṃ yena nipītaṃ
paramapadaṃ khalu tena gṛhītam
mātargaṅge tvayi yo bhaktaḥ
kila taṃ draṣṭuṃ na yamaśśaktaḥ (4)

tava - your; *jalam* - waters; *amalam* - pure; *yena* - by whom; *nipītam* - is drunk; *parama-padam* - the supreme abode; *khalu* - indeed; *tena* - by him; *gṛhītam* - gained; *mātaḥ* - O Mother!; *gaṅge* - O *Gaṅgā*!; *tvayi* - in you; *yaḥ* - who; *bhaktaḥ* - devotee; *kila* - certainly; *tam* - him; *draṣṭum* - to see; *na* - not; *yamaḥ* - Lord *Yama*; *śaktaḥ* - is capable

O Mother *Gaṅgā*! your waters are pure. The one who drinks your waters definitely gains the supreme abode. Lord *Yama* is certainly incapable of even looking at one who has devotion in you.

पतितोद्धारिणि जाह्नवि गङ्गे ó
खण्डितगिरिवरमण्डितभङ्गे ।
भीष्मजननि हे मुनिवरकन्ये
पतितनिवारणि त्रिभुवनधन्ये॥ ५॥

patitoddhāriṇi jāhnavi gaṅge
khaṇḍitagirivaramaṇḍitabhaṅge
bhīṣmajanani he munivarakanye
patitanivāriṇi tribhuvanadhanye (5)

patitoddhāriṇi - the one who uplifts the fallen; *jāhnavi* - daughter of Sage *Jahnu*; *gaṅge* - O *Gaṅgā*!; *khaṇḍita-girivara-maṇḍita-bhaṅge* - one who is adorned with waves that constantly dash against the boulders of the great mountain; *bhīṣma-janani* - mother of *Bhīṣma*; *he munivara-kanye* - O daughter of the great sage; *patita-nivāriṇi* - one who rescues the fallen; *tribhuvana-dhanye* - who is the blessed one in all the three worlds

O *Gaṅgā*! the daughter of the great sage *Jahnu* and mother of *Bhīṣma*, who indeed is blessed one in all the three worlds and who is adorned with waves that constantly dash against the boulders of the great mountain (the *Himālayas*), you are the one who uplift the fallen ones.

कल्पलतामिव फलदां लोके ó
प्रणमति यस्त्वां न पतति शोके ।
पारावारविहारिणि गङ्गे ó
विमुखयुवतिकृततरलापाङ्गे॥ ६॥

kalpalatāmiva phaladāṃ loke
praṇamati yastvāṃ na patati śoke
pārāvāravihāriṇi gaṅge
vimukhayuvatikṛtataralāpāṅge (6)

kalpa-latām - the wish-fulfilling creeper; *iva* - like; *phaladām* - one who gives the desired objects; *loke* - in the world; *praṇamati* - prostrates; *yaḥ* - who; *tvām* - you; *na* - not; *patati* - falls; *śoke* - in sorrow; *pārāvāra-vihāriṇi* - one who sports between the two banks; *gaṅge* - O *Gaṅgā*!; *vimukha-yuvatikṛta-taralāpāṅge* - the one who has an unsteady glance like a forlorn young woman

O *Gaṅgā*! the one who ever sports between the two banks and who has an unsteady glance like a forlorn young woman in this world, sorrow does not befall the one, who salutes you who are like the wish-fulfilling creeper.

तवचेन्मातस्स्रोतस्नातः
पुनरपि जठरे सोऽपि न जातः ।
नरकनिवारिणि जाह्नवि गङ्गे
कलुषविनाशिनि महिमोत्तुङ्गे ॥ ७॥

tavacenmātassrotasnātaḥ
punarapi jaṭare so'pi na jātaḥ
narakanivāriṇi jāhnavi gaṅge
kaluṣavināśini mahimottuṅge (7)

tava - your; *cet* - if; *mātaḥ* - O Mother!; *srotaḥ* - waters; *snātaḥ* - bathed; *punaḥ* - again; *api* - also; *jaṭare* - in the womb; *saḥ* - he; *api* - indeed; *na* - not; *jātaḥ* - is born; *naraka-nivāriṇi* - who rescues from the hell; *jāhnavi* - daughter of *Jahnu*; *gaṅge* - O *Gaṅgā*!; *kaluṣa-vināśini* - who destroys the results of wrong actions; *mahimottuṅge* - whose glories stand high

O Mother *Gaṅgā*! *Jāhnavi*! the one who rescues (people) from hell and destroys the results of (their) wrong actions and whose glories stand high, whoever takes a dip in your waters is never born again in the womb.

पुनरसदङ्गे पुण्यतरङ्गे
जय जय जाह्नवि करुणापाङ्गे।
इन्द्रमुकुटमणिराजितचरणे
सुखदे शुभदे भृत्यशरण्ये ॥८॥

punarasadaṅge puṇyataraṅge
jaya jaya jāhnavi karuṇāpāṅge
indramukuṭamaṇirājitacaraṇe
sukhade śubhade bhṛtyaśaraṇye (8)

punaḥ - again; *asadaṅge* - in the impure limbs; *puṇya-taraṅge* - the one with waves that are pure; *jaya jaya* - victory unto you, victory unto you; *jāhnavi* - O *Jāhnavi*; *karuṇāpāṅge* - who has a compassionate glance; *indra-mukuṭa-maṇi-rājita-caraṇe* - whose feet are resplendent with the jewels of the crown of *Indra*; *sukhade* - who gives happiness; *śubhade* - who gives auspiciousness; *bhṛtya-śaraṇye* - the giver of refuge to those who serve you

O *Jāhnavi*! the one with pure waves uniting with my impure limbs, who has a compassionate glance, whose feet are resplendent with the jewels of the crown of *Indra*, who is a refuge to those who serve, and who gives happiness and prosperity, victory unto you, victory unto you!

रोगं शोकं तापं पापं
हर मे भगवति कुमतिकलापम् ।
त्रिभुवनसारे वसुधाहारेú
त्वमसि गतिर्मम खलु संसारे ।। ९ ।।

rogaṃ śokaṃ tāpaṃ pāpaṃ
hara me bhagavati kumatikalāpam
tribhuvanasāre vasudhāhāre
tvamasi gatirmama khalu saṃsāre (9)

rogam - disease, *śokam* - sorrow; *tāpam* - regret; *pāpam* - wrong deeds; *hara* - take away; *me* - my; *bhagavati* - O *Bhagavati*!; *kumati-kalāpam* - the host of wrong thoughts; *tribhuvanasāre* - who is the essence of the three worlds; *vasudhā-hāre* - who is the necklace of the earth; *tvam* - you; *asi* - are; *gatiḥ* - refuge; *mama* - my; *khalu* - indeed; *saṃsāre* - in the world of limited existence

O *Bhagavati*! who is the essence of the three worlds and the necklace of the earth, may you destroy my disease (of ignorance), sorrow, regret, wrong deeds and the host of wrong thoughts. In *saṃsāra*, you are indeed my refuge.

अलकानन्दे परमानन्दे ú
कुरु करुणां मयि कातरवन्द्ये ।
तव तटनिकटे यस्य निवासः
खलु वैकुण्ठे तस्य निवासः ।। १० ।।

alakānande paramānande
kuru karuṇāṃ mayi kātaravandye
tava taṭanikaṭe yasya nivāsaḥ
khalu vaikuṇṭhe tasya nivāsaḥ (10)

alakānande - O one who gives joy to the people of *Alakāpuri*; *paramānande* - who is the embodiment of happiness; *kuru* - may you show; *karuṇām* - compassion; *mayi* - in me; *kātaravandye* - who is worshipped by the distressed; *tava* - your; *taṭa-nikaṭe* - near the bank; *yasya* - whose; *nivāsaḥ* - residence; *khalu* - indeed; *vaikuṇṭhe* - in *Vaikuṇṭhe*; *tasya* - his; *nivāsaḥ* - dwelling

O one who gives joy to the people of *Alakāpuri*! one who is the embodiment of happiness and who is worshipped by the distressed, whoever lives near your bank indeed lives in *Vaikuṇṭha* alone. May you show compassion in me.

वरमिह नीरे कमठो मीनः
किं वा तीरे शरटः क्षीणः।
अथवा श्वपचो मलिनो दीनस्
तव नहि दूरे नृपतिकुलीनः ॥ ११ ॥

varamihanīre kamaṭho mīnaḥ
kiṃ vā tīre śaraṭaḥ kṣīṇaḥ
athavā śvapaco malino dīnas
tava nahi dūre nṛpatikulīnaḥ (11)

varam - better; *iha* - here; *nīre* - in the waters; *kamaṭhaḥ* - tortoise; *mīnaḥ* - fish; *kiṃ vā* - or else; *tīre* - on the bank; *śaraṭaḥ* - chameleon; *kṣīṇaḥ* - weak; *athavā* - or else; *śvapacaḥ* - one who cooks dogs; *malinaḥ* - dirty; *dīnaḥ* - poor; *tava* - your; *na* - not; *hi* - indeed; *dūre* - far away; *nṛpatikulīnaḥ* - king of high descent

O *Devi*! it is better to live in your waters here as a tortoise or a fish, or else as a weak chameleon on your bank or even as a dirty, poor *caṇḍāla* (person of low conduct) near your bank, than as a king of high descent away from you.

भो भुवनेश्वरि पुण्ये धन्ये
देवि द्रवमयि मुनिवरकन्ये ।
गङ्गास्तवमिमममलं नित्यं
पठति नरो यस्स जयति सत्यम् ॥ १२ ॥

bho bhuvaneśvari puṇye dhanye
devi dravamayi munivarakanye
gaṅgāstavamimamamalaṃ nityaṃ
paṭhati naro yassa jayati satyam (12)

bho bhuvaneśvari - O the ruler of the universe!; *puṇye* - who is holy; *dhanye* - who is blessed; *devi* - O *Devi*!; *dravamayi* - who is in the form of waters; *munivara-kanye* - daughter of great sage; *gaṅgā-stavam* - the hymn of *Gaṅgā*; *imam* - this; *amalam* - pure; *nityam* - daily; *paṭhati* - recites; *naraḥ* - person; *yaḥ* - who; *saḥ* - he; *jayati* - wins; *satyam* - definitely

O *Bhuvaneśvari*! O *Devi*! one who is in the form of waters, who is holy, who is blessed and who is the daughter of a great sage, whoever daily recites this pure hymn of *Gaṅgā*, definitely succeeds in life.

येषां हृदये गङ्गाभक्तिस्-
तेषां भवति सदा सुखमुक्तिः।
मधुराकान्तापज्झटिकाभिः
परमानन्दकलितललिताभिः ॥१३॥

yeṣāṃ hṛdaye gaṅgābhaktis-
teṣāṃ bhavati sadā sukhamuktiḥ
madhurākāntāpajjhaṭikhābhiḥ
paramānandakalitalalitābhiḥ (13)

yeṣām- of whose; *hṛdaye* - in the heart; *gaṅgā-bhaktis* - there is devotion for *Gaṅgā*; *teṣām* - for them; *bhavati* - happens; *sadā* - always; *sukhamuktiḥ* - effortless freedom; *madhurākāntā-pajjhaṭikhābhiḥ* - by this hymn which is in simple meter known as *pajjhaṭikhā* and which is sweet and attractive; *paramānanda-kalita-lalitābhiḥ* - which is an elegant composition full of joy

He, who has devotion for *Gaṅgā* in his heart, always gains effortless freedom by the recitation of this hymn, which is in a simple meter, sweet and attractive, and which is an elegant composition full of joy.

गङ्गास्तोत्रमिदं भवसारं ú
वाञ्छितफलदं विमलं सारम् ।
शङ्करसेवकशङ्कररचितं
पठति सुखी स्तव इति च समाप्तः ॥१४॥

gaṅgāstotramidaṃ bhavasāraṃ
vañchitaphaladaṃ vimalaṃ sāram
śaṅkarasevakaśaṅkararacitaṃ
paṭhati sukhī stava iti ca samāptaḥ (14)

gaṅgā-stotram - the hymn of *Gaṅgā*; *idam* - this; *bhava-sāram-* which is the essence of this universe; *vañchita-phaladam* - which gives desired results; *vimalam* - pure; *sāram* - the truth; *śaṅkara-sevaka-śaṅkara-racitaṃ* - which is composed by *Śrī Śaṅkara* who is a devotee of Lord *Śiva*; *paṭhati* - recites; *sukhī* - he gains happiness; *stavaḥ* - hymn; *iti* - thus; *ca* - and; *samāptaḥ* - ends

This hymn of *Gaṅgā* is the essence of this universe. It gives one, the desired results. It is pure and contains the truth. One, who recites this hymn, composed by *Śrī Śaṅkara*, who is a devotee of Lord *Śiva*, gains happiness. Thus ends the hymn.

जय जय गङ्गे जय हर गङ्गे ó जय जय गङ्गे जय हर गङ्गे।
जय जय गङ्गे जय हर गङ्गे ó जय जय गङ्गे जय हर गङ्गे।। ó
जय जय गङ्गे जय हर गङ्गे ó जय जय गङ्गे जय हर गङ्गे।
जय जय गङ्गे जय हर गङ्गे ó जय जय गङ्गे जय हर गङ्गे।। ó
जय जय गङ्गे जय हर गङ्गे ó जय जय गङ्गे जय हर गङ्गे।।

jaya jaya gaṅge jaya hara gaṅge
jaya jaya gaṅge jaya hara gaṅge
jaya jaya gaṅge jaya hara gaṅge
jaya jaya gaṅge jaya hara gaṅge
jaya jaya gaṅge jaya hara gaṅge
jaya jaya gaṅge jaya hara gaṅge
jaya jaya gaṅge jaya hara gaṅge
jaya jaya gaṅge jaya hara gaṅge
jaya jaya gaṅge jaya hara gaṅge
jaya jaya gaṅge jaya hara gaṅge

jaya-jaya - victory unto you; *gaṅge* - O *Gaṅgā*!; *jaya* - victory unto you; *hara* - remove (my *pāpas*); *gaṅge* - O *Gaṅgā*!

O *Gaṅgā*! victory unto you! O *Gaṅgā*! remove my *pāpas*.

श्री गङ्गामय्या की जय

śrī gaṅgāmayyā kī jay
Victory unto Mother *Gaṅgā*

Part 8

Śāradā Stotram

नमस्ते शारदे देवि काश्मीरपुरवासिनि ।
त्वामहं प्रार्थये नित्यं विद्यादानं च देहि मे ॥१॥

namaste śārade devi kāśmīrapuravāsini
tvāmahaṃ prārthaye nityaṃ vidyādānaṃ ca dehi me (1)

namaḥ - salutation; *te* - to you; *śārade* - O *Sarasvatī*!; *devi* - O *Devi*!; *kāśmīra-puravāsini* - one who resides in the city of Kashmir; *tvām* - you; *aham* - I; *prārthaye* - pray to; *nityam* - always; *vidyā-dānam* - gift of knowledge; *ca* - and; *dehi* - give; *me* - to me

O Goddess *Sarasvatī* in the shrine of *Śāradā Pīṭha* in Kashmir, I offer my salutation to you. I pray always to you to give me the gift of knowledge.

या श्रद्धा धारणा मेधा वाग्देवी विधिवल्लभा ।
भक्तजिह्वाग्रसदना शमादिगुणदायिनि ॥२॥

yā śraddhā dhāraṇā medhā vagdevīvidhivallabhā
bhaktajihvāgrasadanā śamādiguṇadāyini (2)

yā - which; *śraddhā* - faith; *dhāraṇā* - the power of retention; *medhā* - the power of memory; *vagdevī* - goddess of speech; *vidhi-vallabhā* - the consort of Lord *Brahmā*; *bhakta-jihvāgra-sadanā* - the one who dwells at the tip of the tongue of devotees; *śamādi-guṇa-dāyini* - O one who grants qualities like mastery over the mind

O one who grants qualities like mastery over the mind (to your devotees)! you are the faith, the power of retention (of what is learned) and the power of memory. You are the goddess of speech. You are the consort of Lord *Brahmā*. You dwell at the tip of the tongue of devotees.

नमामि यामिनीं नाथलेखालङ्कृतकुन्तलाम्।
भवानीं भवसन्तापनिर्वापणसुधानदीम् ॥३॥

namāmi yāminīṃ nāthalekhālaṅkṛtakuntalām
bhavānīṃ bhavasantāpanirvāpaṇasudhānadīm (3)

namāmi - I salute; *yāminīm* - the one who has mastery of everything; *nātha-lekhālaṅkṛta-kuntalām* - one whose hair is done to the liking of Lord *Brahmā*; *bhavānīm* - *Pārvatī*; *bhava-santāpa-nirvāpaṇa-sudhā-nadīm* - one who is the river of nectar that extinguishes the fire of the afflictions of *saṃsāra*

I salute you, who has mastery of everything, whose hair is done to the liking of Lord *Brahmā*, who is *Pārvatī* and who is the river of nectar (knowledge) that extinguishes the fire of the afflictions of *saṃsāra*.

भद्रकाल्यै नमो नित्यं सरस्वत्यै नमो नमः।
वेदवेदाङ्गवेदान्तविद्यास्थानेभ्य एव च॥ ४॥

bhadrakālyai namo nityaṃ sarasvatyai namo namaḥ
vedavedāṅgavedāntavidyāsthānebhya eva ca (4)

bhadrakālyai - to Goddess *Durgā*; *namaḥ* - salutation; *nityam* - always; *sarasvatyai* - to Goddess *Sarasvatī*; *namaḥ namaḥ* - repeated salutations; *veda-vedāṅga-vedānta-vidyāsthānebhya* - to the abode of knowledge such as *veda*, *vedāṅgas* and *Vedānta*; *eva ca* - also

My salutation to Goddess *Durgā* always. My repeated salutations to Goddess *Sarasvatī* who is the abode of knowledge such as *Vedas*, *Vedāṅgas* and *Upaniṣads*.

ब्रह्मस्वरूपा परमा ज्योतिरूपा सनातनी।
सर्वविद्याधिदेवी या तस्यै वाण्यै नमो नमः॥ ५॥

brahmasvarūpā paramā jyotirūpā sanātanī
sarvavidyādhidevī yā tasyai vāṇyai namo namaḥ (5)

brahmasvarūpā - whose nature is *Brahman*; *paramā* - who is supreme; *jyotirūpā* - whose form is the light of knowledge; *sanātanī* - eternal; *sarva-vidyā-adhidevī* - the presiding deity of all knowledge; *yā* - who; *tasyai* - to her; *vāṇyai* - to *Sarasvatī*; *namaḥ namaḥ* - repeated salutations

My repeated salutations to *Sarasvatī* whose nature is *Brahman*, who is supreme, whose form is the light of knowledge, who is the presiding deity of all knowledge and who is eternal.

यया विना जगत्सर्वं शश्वज्जीवन्मृतं भवेत्।
ज्ञानाधिदेवी या तस्यै सरस्वत्यै नमो नमः॥ ६॥

yayā vinā jagatsarvaṃ śaśvajjīvanmṛtaṃ bhavet
jñānādhidevī yā tasyai sarasvatyai namo namaḥ (6)

yayā vinā - without whom; *jagatsarvam* - the entire world; *śaśvat* - for ever; *jīvan*- living; *mṛtaṃ* - dead; *bhavet* - would become; *jñānādhidevī* - who is the presiding deity of knowledge; *yā* - who; *tasyai* - to her; *sarasvatyai* - to *Sarasvatī*; *nama□nama□*- my repeated salutations

My repeated salutations to Goddess *Sarasvatī*, who is the presiding deity of knowledge and without whom the entire world of living beings would become like dead forever.

यया विना जगत्सर्वं मूकमुन्मत्तवत् सदा।
या देवी वागधिष्ठात्री तस्यै वाण्यै नमो नमः ।। ७ ।।

yayā vinā jagatsarvaṃ mūkamunmattavat sadā
yā devī vāgadhiṣṭhātrī tasyai vāṇyai namo namaḥ (7)

yayā vinā - without whom; *jagatsarvam* - the entire world; *mūkam* - dumb; *unmattavat* - like mad; *sadā* - always; *yā* - who; *devī* - goddess; *vāk-adhiṣṭhātrī* - the presiding deity of speech; *tasyai* - to her; *vāṇyai* - to *Sarasvatī*; *namaḥ namaḥ*- repeated salutations

My repeated salutations to Goddess *Sarasvatī* who is the presiding deity of speech, without whom the entire world would be like mute and mad forever

Ārati Mantras

।   ॥

ॐ राजाधिराजाय प्रसह्यसाहिने ।
नमो वयं वैश्रवणाय कुर्महे । ॥
स मे कामान् कामकामाय मह्यम् ।
कामेश्वरो वैश्रवणो ददातु।
कुबेराय वैश्रवणाय ।
महाराजाय नमः ॥१॥

oṃ rājādhirājāya prasahyasāhine
namo vayaṃ vai śravaṇāya kurmahe
sa me kāmān kāmakāmāya mahyam
kāmeśvaro vai śravaṇo dadātu
kuberāya vai śravaṇāya
mahārājāya namaḥ (1)

rājādhirājāya - one who is the king of kings; *prasahyasāhine* - who commands everyone's possessions by his power; *namaḥ* - salutation; *vayam* - we; *vaiśravaṇāya* - to the son of *Viśravas*; *kurmahe* - do; *saḥ* - he; *me* - my; *kāmān* - desired objects; *kāmakāmāya* - to the one who seeks fulfillment of desires; *mahyam* - to me; *kāmeśvaraḥ* - the Lord of desires; *vaiśravaṇaḥ* - *Kubera* (deity of wealth); *dadātu* - let him give; *kuberāya* - to *Kubera*; *vaiśravaṇāya* - to the son of *Viśravas*; *mahārājāya* - to the great king; *namaḥ* - salutation

We offer (our) salutations to *Kubera*, the son of *Viśravas*, who is the king of kings, and who commands everyone's possessions by his power. Let that *Kubera*, the Lord of desires, give the desired objects to me, who is seeking fulfillment of desires. Salutations to *Kubera*, the son of *Viśravas*, the great king.

Mantra Puṣpam - 1

योऽपां पुष्पं वेद।
पुष्पवान् प्रजावान् पशुमान् भवति ।
चन्द्रमा वा अपां पुष्पम् ।
पुष्पवान् प्रजावान् पशुमान् भवति ।
य एवं वेद । योऽपामायतनं वेद ।
आयतनवान् भवति ॥ २॥

yo'pāṃ puṣpaṃ veda
puṣpavān prajāvān paśumān bhavati
candramā vā apāṃ puṣpam
puṣpavān prajāvan paśumān bhavati
ya evaṃ veda yo'pāmāyatanaṃ veda
āyatanavān bhavati (2)

yaḥ - the one who; *apām* - of the Lord; *puṣpam* - the flower (emerging out); *veda* - knows; *puṣpavān* - endowed with flowers; *prajāvān* - endowed with progeny; *paśumān* - endowed with cattle; *bhavati* - becomes; *candramāḥ vai* - moon alone is; *apām* - of the Lord; *puṣpam* - the flower (emerging out); *puṣpavān* - endowed with flowers; *prajāvān* - endowed with progeny; *paśumān* - endowed with cattle; *bhavati* - becomes; *yaḥ* - the one who; *evam* - thus; *veda* - knows; *yaḥ* - the one who; *apām* - of the Lord; *āyatanam* - the support; *veda* - knows; *āyatanavān* - endowed with support; *bhavati* - becomes

The one who knows the flower (emerging out) of the Lord, becomes (endowed with) flowers, progeny and cattle; the moon is indeed the flower (emerging out) of the Lord; the one who knows thus becomes endowed with flowers, progeny and cattle; the one who knows the support of the Lord, becomes endowed with support.

Mantra Puṣpam - 2

ओं तद्ब्रह्म। ओं तद्वायुः। ओं तदात्मा।
ओं तत्सत्यम्। ओं तत्सर्वम्। ओं तत्पुरोर्नमः।
आन्तश्चरति भूतेषु गुहायां विश्वमूर्त्तिषु।
त्वं यज्ञस्त्वं वषड्कारस्त्वमिन्द्रस्त्व रुद्रस्त्वं विष्णुस्त्वं ब्रह्म त्वं प्रजापतिः।
त्वं तदाप आपो ज्योती रसोऽमृतं ब्रह्म भूर्भुवस्सुवरोम्॥ ३॥

oṃ tadbrahma / oṃ tadvāyuḥ / oṃ tadātmā
oṃ tatsatyam / oṃ tatsarvam / oṃ tatpurornamaḥ
antaścarati bhūteṣu guhāyāṃ viśvamūrttiṣu
tvaṃ yajñastvaṃ vaṣatkārastvamindrastvam̐
rudrastvaṃ viṣṇustvaṃ brahma tvaṃ prajāpatiḥ
tvaṃ tadāpa āpo jyoti raso'mṛtaṃ brahma bhūrbhuvassuvarom (3)

om - that which is understood by *om*; *tat* - that; *brahma* - (is) *Brahman*; *om* - that which is understood by *om*; *tat* - that; *vāyuḥ* - (is) *hiraṇyagarbha*; *om* - that which is understood by *om*; *tat* - that; *ātmā* - (is) *jīva*, the soul; *om* - that which is understood by *om*; *tat* - that; *satyam* - (is) the ultimate truth; *om* - that which is understood by *om*; *tat* - that; *sarvam* - (is) everything; *om* - that which is understood by *om*; *tat* - that; *puroḥ* - of all bodies outside; *namaḥ* - (unto that *Brahman*); salutation; *antaḥ* - inside; *carati* - moves; *bhūteṣu* - in the beings; *guhāyām* - in the intellect; *viśvamūrttiṣu* - in all forms; *tvam* - you; *yajñaḥ* - (are) the sacrifice; *tvam* - you; *vaṣatkāraḥ*- (are) the expression '*vaṣaṭ*' used while offering oblations; *tvam* - you; *indraḥ* - (are) *Indra*; *tvam* - you; *rudraḥ* - (are) *Rudra*; *tvam* - you; *viṣṇuḥ* - (are) *Viṣṇu*; *tvam* - you; *brahma* - (are) *Brahmā*; *tvam* - you; *prajāpatiḥ* - (are) *Prajāpati*; *tvam* - you; *tat* - (are) that; *āpaḥ* - waters (in the rivers); *āpaḥ* - waters (in the ocean); *jyotiḥ* - the light (in the luminaries); *rasaḥ* - the taste (such as sweet); *amṛtaṃ* - essence of everything; *brahma* - the body of *Vedas*; *bhūrbhuvassuvaḥ* - the threefold worlds; *om* - *omkāra*

Om is that *Brahman*. That is *Hiraṇyagarbha*, the total. That is the individual *jīva*. That is the ultimate truth. That is everything. Salutations unto that *Brahman* who is the outside world. That truth obtains in the intellect of all beings in their different forms. You are the sacrifice and the expression '*vaṣaṭ*' (used in the sacrifice). You are *Indra, Rudra, Viṣṇu, Brahmā, Prajāpati* and the self. You are the waters in the rivers and oceans, the light in the luminaries, the tastes in food, the essence of everything, the body of the *Vedas*, the threefold worlds and *Om*.

Prātaḥ Smaraṇam

प्रातस्स्मरामि हृदि संस्फुरदात्मतत्वं
सच्चित्सुखं परमहंसगतिं तुरीयम् ।
यत्स्वप्नजागरसुषुप्तमवैति नित्यं
तद्ब्रह्म निष्कलमहं न च भूतसङ्घः ॥१॥

prātassmarāmi hṛdi saṃsphuradātmatatvaṃ
saccitsukhaṃ paramahaṃsagatiṃ turīyam
yatsvapnajāgarasuṣuptamavaiti nityaṃ
tadbrahma niṣkalamahaṃ na ca bhūtasaṅgaḥ (1)

prātaḥ- early morning; *smarāmi* - I remember; *hṛdi* - in the heart; *saṃsphurat* - shining; *ātma-tatvam* - the truth of self; *saccitsukham* - that ever present limitless awareness; *parama-haṃsa-gatim* - the supreme goal of *sannyāsīs*; *turīyam* - known as the fourth; *yat* - which; *svapna-jāgara-suṣuptam* - in dream, waking and sleep; *avaiti* - witnesses; *nityam* - always; *tat* - that; *brahma* - *Brahman*; *niṣkalam* - undivided; *aham* - I; *na ca* - and not; *bhūta-saṅgaḥ*- aggregate of elements

Early morning, I remember the shining truth of the self in the heart, that which is ever present, limitless awareness, the supreme goal of *sannyāsīs*, known as the 'fourth', and which always witnesses dream, waking and deep sleep. I am that undivided *Brahman* and not an aggregate of elements.

प्रातर्भजामि मनसा वचसामगम्यं
वाचो विभान्ति निखिला यदनुग्रहेण ।
यं नेति नेति वचनैर्निगमा अवोचुः
तं देवदेवमजमच्युतमाहुरग्र्यम् ॥२॥

prātarbhajāmi manasā vacasāmagamyaṃ
vāco vibhānti nikhilā yadanugraheṇa
yaṃ neti neti vacanairnigamā avocuḥ
taṃ devadevamajamacyutamāhuragryam (2)

prātaḥ - early morning; *bhajāmi* - I worship; *manasā* - by the mind; *vacasām* - of the speech; *agamyam* - inconceivable; *vācaḥ* - words; *vibhānti* - manifest; *nikhilāḥ* - entire; *yat* - whose; *anugraheṇa* - by blessing; *yam* - which; *neti* - 'not this'; *neti* - 'not this'; *vacanaiḥ* - by the words; *nigamāḥ* - *Vedas*; *avocuḥ* - described; *tam* - that; *devadevam* - the Lord of deities; *ajam* - unborn; *acyutam* - changeless; *āhuḥ* - they say; *agryam* - the foremost

Early morning, I worship him in the mind who cannot be conceived by speech, by whose blessing all the words are manifest and whom the *Vedas* described by the words 'not this, not this'. That one, they say, is the foremost, the Lord of the deities, the unborn and changeless.

प्रातर्नमामि तमसः परमर्कवर्णं
पूर्णं सनातनपदं पुरुषोत्तमाख्यम्।
यस्मिन्निदं जगदशेषमशेषमूर्त्तौ
रज्ज्वां भुजङ्गम इव प्रतिभासितं वै ॥३॥

prātarnamāmi tamasaḥ paramarkavarṇaṃ
pūrṇaṃ sanātanapadaṃ puruṣottamākhyam
yasminnidaṃ jagadaśeṣamaśeṣamūrttau
rajjvāṃ bhujaṅgama iva pratibhāsitaṃ vai (3)

prātaḥ- early morning; *namāmi* - I bow; *tamasaḥ* - from darkness; *param* - beyond; *arka-varṇam* - has the lustre of the sun; *pūrṇam* - limitless; *sanātanapadam* - changeless support; *puruṣottamākhyam* - known as the supreme being; *yasmin* - in whom; *idam* - this; *jagat* - universe; *aśeṣam* - the entire; *aśeṣamūrttau* - in the limitless form; *rajjvām* - in a rope; *bhujaṅgamaḥ iva* - like a snake; *pratibhāsitam* - has appeared; *vai* - indeed

Early morning, I bow to the limitless, that which is beyond darkness, which has the lustre of the sun, which is the changeless support known as the supreme being, in whose limitless form the entire universe has appeared like a snake upon a rope.

Śānti Mantras

ॐ सह नाववतु। सह नौ भुनक्तु।
सह वीर्यं करवावहै। तेजस्विनावधीतमस्तु।।
मा विद्विषावहै।। ॐ शान्तिः शान्तिः शान्तिः ।।१।।

oṃ sa ha nāvavatu / sa ha nau bhunaktu
sa ha vīryaṃ karavāvahai / tejasvināvadhītamastu
mā vidviṣāvahai / oṃ śāntiḥ śāntiḥ śāntiḥ (1)

saḥ - he; *ha* - indeed; *nau* - both of us; *avatu* - may protect; *saḥ* - he; *ha* - indeed; *nau* - both of us; *bhunaktu* - may nourish; *saha* - together; *vīryaṃ karavāvahai* - may we acquire the capacity (to study and understand the scriptures); *tejasvi* - brilliant; *nau* - for us; *adhītam* - what is studied; *astu* - let it be; *mā vidviṣāvahai* - may we not disagree with each other; *oṃ śāntiḥ śāntiḥ śāntiḥ* - *om* peace, peace, peace

May the Lord indeed, protect both of us. May he indeed, nourish both of us. May we together acquire the capacity (to study and understand the scriptures). May our study be brilliant. May we not disagree with each other. *om* peace, peace, peace.

ॐ शन्नो मित्रः शं वरुणः। शन्नो भवत्वर्यमा ।
शन्न इन्द्रो बृहस्पतिः ।शन्नो विष्णुरुरुक्रमः।
नमो ब्रह्मणे । नमस्ते वायो। त्वमेव प्रत्यक्षं ब्रह्मासि ।
त्वमेव प्रत्यक्षं ब्रह्म वदिष्यामि। ऋतं वदिष्यामि ।
सत्यं वदिष्यामि।। तन्मामवतु। तद्वक्तारमवतु । अवतु
माम्। अवतु वक्तारम्।। अवतु वक्तारम् ।। ॐ शान्तिः शान्तिः शान्तिः ।।२।।

oṃ śanno mitraḥ śaṃ varuṇaḥ / śanno bhavatvaryamā
śanna indro bṛhaspatiḥ / śanno viṣṇururukramaḥ
namo brahmaṇe / namaste vāyo / tvameva pratyakṣaṃ brahmāsi
tvameva pratyakṣaṃ brahma vadiṣyāmi / ṛtaṃ vadiṣyāmi
satyaṃ vadiṣyāmi / tanmāmavatu / tadvaktāramavatu
avatu mām / avatu vaktāram / oṃ śāntiḥ śāntiḥ śāntiḥ (2)

śam - auspiciousness; *naḥ* - to us; *mitraḥ* - the sun deity; *śam* - auspiciousness; *varuṇaḥ* - the ocean deity; *śam* - auspiciousness; *naḥ* - to us; *bhavatu* - let (him) be; *aryamā* - lord of the manes; *śam* - auspiciousness; *naḥ* - to us; *indraḥ* - the ruler of *devatās*; *bṛhaspatiḥ* - the preceptor of *devatās*; *śam* - auspiciousness; *naḥ* - to us; *viṣṇuḥ* - the all pervasive sustainer of creation; *urukramaḥ* - the cosmic Lord; *namaḥ* - salutation; *brahmaṇe* - to the creator; *namaḥ* - salutation; *te* - to you; *vāyo* - O deity of wind; *tvam eva* - you indeed; *pratyakṣam* - perceptible; *brahma* - the truth; *asi* - are; *tvam eva* - you indeed; *pratyakṣam* - perceptible; *brahma* - the truth; *vadiṣyāmi* - I declare (understand); *ṛtaṃ* - proper understanding; *vadiṣyāmi* - I declare (understand); *satyam* - truthfulness in speech; *vadiṣyāmi* - I declare (understand); *tat* - it; *mām* - me; *avatu* - may protect; *tat* - it; *vaktāram* - the teacher; *avatu* - may protect; *avatu* - may protect; *mām* - me ; *avatu* - may protect; *vaktāram* - the teacher; *oṃ śāntiḥ śāntiḥ śāntiḥ* - *om* peace, peace, peace

May the sun deity give us auspiciousness. May the ocean deity give us auspiciousness. May the lord of manes give us auspiciousness. May the ruler of *devatās* and the preceptor of *devatās* give us auspiciousness. May the all pervasive sustainer of creation, Lord *Vāmana*, give us auspiciousness. Salutations to the creator. Salutations to you, O deity of wind! You indeed are the perceptible truth. I understand you to be the perceptible truth. I declare you to be the right understanding. I understand you to be the truthfulness in speech. May the truth protect me. May the truth protect the teacher. May the truth protect me. May the truth protect the teacher. *Om* peace, peace, peace.

ॐ यश्छन्द॑सामृष॒भो वि॒श्वरू॑पः। छन्दो॒भ्योऽध्य॒मृता᳚त् संब॒भूव॑।
स मेन्द्रो॑ मे॒धया᳚ स्पृणोतु। अ॒मृत॑स्य देव॒ धार॑णो भूयासम्।
शरी॑रं मे॒ विच॑र्षणम्। जि॒ह्वा मे॒ मधु॑मत्तमा।
कर्णा᳚भ्या॒ं भूरि॒ विश्रु॑वम्। ब्रह्म॑णः को॒शो॑ऽसि मे॒धया॒ पिहि॑तः।
श्रु॒तं मे॑ गोपाय। ॐ शान्ति॒ः शान्ति॒ः शान्ति॑ः॥ ३॥

oṃ yaśchandasāmṛṣabho viśvarūpaḥ / chandobhyo'dhyamṛtāt sambabhūva
sa mendro medhayā spṛṇotu / amṛtasya deva dhāraṇo bhūyāsam
śarīraṃ me vicarṣaṇam / jihvā me madhumattamā
karṇābhyāṃ bhūri viśruvam / brahmaṇaḥ kośo'si medhayā pihitaḥ
śrutaṃ me gopāya / oṃ śāntiḥ śāntiḥ śāntiḥ (3)

yaḥ - that (*oṃkāra*); *chandasām* - among the Vedic *mantras*; *ṛsabhaḥ* - is the greatest; *viśvarūpaḥ* - is endowded with all forms; *chandobhyaḥ* - from the *Vedas*; *amṛtāt* - which are eternal; *adhi- sambabhūva* - came into being; *saḥ* - that; *mā* - me; *indraḥ* - *Indra*, the Lord; *medhayā* - with intelligence; *spṛṇotu* - strengthen; *amṛtasya* - of that knowledge which is eternal; *deva* - O Lord! *dhāraṇaḥ* - the upholder; *bhūyāsam* - let me become; *śarīram* - body; *me* - my; *vicarṣaṇam* - be healthy; *jihvā* - tongue; *me* - my; *madhumattamā* - be the sweetest; *karṇābhyām* - through (my ears); *bhūri* - more and more; *viśruvam* - let me listen (to the scriptures); *brahmaṇaḥ* - of *Brahman*; *kośaḥ* - the abode; *asi* - you are; *medhayā* - by knowledge (of objects); *pihitaḥ* - you are veiled; *śrutam* - what is heard; *me* - by me; *gopāya* - you protect; *oṃ śāntiḥ śāntiḥ śāntiḥ* - *om* peace, peace, peace

That *Oṃkāra* which manifested from the eternal *Vedas* is the greatest among the Vedic *mantras* and is endowed with all forms. Let that Lord (*om*) strengthen me with intelligence. O Lord, let me become the upholder of that knowledge which is eternal. May my physical body become fit for the pursuit of knowledge. Let my tongue be one that speaks pleasing words. May my ears listen to the scriptures more and more. You are the abode of *Brahman*, veiled by the knowledge of objects. May you protect my knowledge. *Om* peace, peace, peace.

ॐ अहं वृक्षसय् रेरिवा । कीर्तिः पृष्ठं गिरेरिव ।
ऊर्ध्वपवित्रो वाजिनीव स्वमृतमस्मि । द्रविण सवर्चसम् ।
सुमेधा अमृतोक्षितः । इति त्रिशङ्कोर्वेदानुवचनम् ।
ॐ शान्तिः शान्तिः शान्तिः ॥ ४ ॥

oṃ ahaṃ vṛkṣasya rerivā / kīrttiḥ pṛṣṭhaṃ gireriva
ūrdhvapavitro vājinīva svamṛtamasmi / draviṇaṁ savarcasam
sumedhā amṛtokṣitaḥ / iti triśaṅkorvedānuvacanam
oṃ śāntiḥ śāntiḥ śāntiḥ (4)

aham - I; *vṛkṣasya* - of the tree (of *saṃsāra*); *rerivā* - am the sustainer; *kīrttiḥ* - (my) fame; *pṛṣṭham* - the peak; *gireḥ* - of a mountain; *iva* - like; *ūrdhvapavitraḥ* - I am absolutely pure; *vājini* - the effulgence in the sun; *iva* - like; *svamṛtam* - the limitless awareness; *asmi* - I am; *draviṇam* - the wealth; *savarcasam* - the most shining (I am); *sumedhāḥ* - the most auspicious knowledge (I am endowded with); *amṛtaḥ*- free from death; *ukṣitaḥ* - free from decay (I am); *iti* - thus; *triśaṅkoḥ* - of Sage *Triśaṅku*; *vedānuvacanam* - is the declaration after the attainment of knowledge; *oṃ śāntiḥ śāntiḥ śāntiḥ* - *om* peace, peace, peace

After gaining self-knowledge Sage *Triśaṅku* declared: "I am the sustainer of the tree of *saṃsāra*. My fame is like the peak of a mountain. I am absolutely pure. I am in the form of pure awareness which is the same as that which obtains in the sun. I am in the form of shining knowledge which is like wealth. I am endowed with the most auspicious knowledge. I am free from death and decay". *Om* peace, peace, peace.

ॐ पुर्णमदः पूर्णमिदं पूर्णात्पूर्णमुदच्यते ।
पूर्णस्य पूर्णमादाय पूर्णमेवावशिष्यते ॥
ॐ शान्तिः शान्तिः शान्तिः ॥ ५ ॥

oṃ pūrṇamadaḥ pūrṇamidaṃ pūrṇātpūrṇamudacyate
pūrṇasya pūrṇamādāya pūrṇamevāvaśiṣyate
oṃ śāntiḥ śāntiḥ śāntiḥ (5)

pūrṇam - is fullness; *adaḥ* - that; *pūrṇam* - is fullness; *idam* - this; *pūrṇāt* - from that fullness; *pūrṇam* - this fullness; *udacyate* - has come; *pūrṇasya* - of that fullness; *pūrṇam* - this fullness; *ādāya* - having removed; *pūrṇam* - the fullness; *eva* - only; *avaśiṣyate* - remains; *oṃ śāntiḥ śāntiḥ śāntiḥ* - *om* peace, peace, peace

That is fullness, this is fullness. From that fullness this fullness came. From that fullness this fullness removed, what remains is fullness. *Om* peace, peace, peace.

ॐ आप्यायन्तु ममाङ्गानि वाक्प्राणश्चक्षुःश्रोत्रमथो
बलमिन्द्रियाणि च सर्वाणि। सर्वं ब्रह्मौपविषदम् ।
माहं ब्रह्म निराकुर्याम्। मा मा ब्रह्म निराकरोत् ।
अनिराकरणमस्त्वनिराकरणं मे अस्तु ।
तदात्मनि निरते य उपनिषत्सु धर्मास् -
ते मयि सन्तु । ते मयि सन्तु ।
ॐ शान्तिः शान्तिः शान्तिः ॥ ६ ॥

oṃ āpyāyantu mamāṅgāni vākprāṇaścakṣuḥśrotramatho
balamindriyāṇi ca sarvāṇi / sarvaṃ brahmaupaniṣadam
mahaṃ brahma nirākuryām / mā mā brahma nirākarot
anirakaraṇamastvanirākaraṇaṃ me astu
tadātmani nirate ya upaniṣatsu dharmās
te mayi santu / te mayi santu
oṃ śāntiḥ śāntiḥ śāntiḥ (6)

āpyāyantu - may they grow (in their power); *mama* - my; *aṅgāni* - limbs; *vāk* - speech; *prāṇaḥ* - vital air; *cakṣuḥ* - eyes; *śrotram* - ears; *atho* - further; *balam* - capacity; *indriyāṇi* - sense organs; *ca* - and; *sarvāṇi* - all; *sarvam* - everything; *brahma* - is *Brahman*; *aupaniṣadam* - that is revealed in the *Upaniṣads*; *mā* - not; *aham* - I; *brahma* - *Brahman*; *nirākuryām* - reject; *mā* - never; *mā* - me; *brahma* - *Brahman*; *nirākarot* - reject; *anirakaraṇam* - non-rejection; *astu* - let there be; *anirākaraṇam* - non-rejection; *me* - for me; *astu* - let there be; *tat* - that; *ātmani* - in the self; *nirate* - in one who revels; *yaḥ* - what; *upaniṣatsu* - in the *Upaniṣads*; *dharmāḥ* - the qualities; *te* - them; *mayi* - in me; *santu* - let them be; *te* - them; *mayi* - in me; *santu* - let them be; *oṃ śāntiḥ śāntiḥ śāntiḥ* - *om* peace, peace, peace

Let all my limbs including speech, vital air, eyes, ears and the other sense organs and my capacity grow in their power. Everything is that *Brahman*, unfolded in the *Upaniṣads*. May I not reject *Brahman* (for lack of *śraddhā*). May not *Brahman*, the Lord, reject me. May there be non-rejection of the Lord by me. May there be non-rejection of the Lord for me. In me who is committed to the pursuit of knowledge of *Brahman*, let there be all those qualities which are mentioned as qualifications in the *Upaniṣads*. Let those qualities be in me. *Om* peace, peace, peace.

ॐ वाङ् मे मनसि प्रतिष्ठिता । मनो मे वाचि प्रतिष्ठितम् ।
आविरावीर्म एधि। वेदस्य म आणीस्थः।
श्रुतं मे मा प्रहासीः। अनेनाधीतेनाहोरात्रान् सन्दधामि।
ऋतं वदिष्यामि। सत्यं वदिष्यामि
तन्मामवतु । तद्वक्तारमवतु ।
अवतु माम्। अवतु वक्तारमवतु वक्तारम् ।
ॐ शान्तिः शान्तिः शान्तिः ॥७॥

oṃ vāṅ me manasi pratiṣṭhitā / mano me vāci pratiṣṭhitam
āvirāvīrmā edhi / vedasya ma āṇīsthaḥ
śrutaṃ me mā prahāsīḥ
anenādhītenāhorātrān sandadhāmi / ṛtaṃ vadiṣyāmi
satyaṃ vadiṣyāmi / tanmāmavatu / tadvaktāramavatu
avatu mām / avatu vaktāramavatu vaktāram
oṃ śāntiḥ śāntiḥ śāntiḥ (7)

vāk- speech; *me* - my; *manasi* - in mind; *pratiṣṭhitā* - let (it) abide; *manaḥ* - mind; *me* - my; *vāci* - in speech; *pratiṣṭhitam* - let (it) abide; *āviḥ* - O self shining *Brahman*; *me* - for me; *āvīḥ edhi* - shine; *vedasya* - of the knowledge; *me* - to me; *āṇīsthaḥ* - (the speech and mind) are capable of bringing; *śrutam*- what is heard; *me* - my; *mā* - not; *prahāsīḥ* - forsake; *anena* - by this; *adhītena* - learning; *ahorātrān* - day and night; *sandadhāmi* - (may I) contemplate upon; *ṛtam* - truth; *vadiṣyāmi* - I speak (understand); *satyam* - that truth; *vadiṣyāmi* - I speak; *tat* - that; *mām* - me; *avatu* - protect; *tat* - that; *vaktāram* - teacher; *avatu* - protect; *avatu* - protect; *mām* - me; *avatu* - protect; *vaktāram* - the teacher; *oṃ śāntiḥ śāntiḥ śāntiḥ* - *om* peace, peace, peace

May my speech be in accord with my mind. Let my mind be in accord with my speech. O self shining *Brahman*! may you reveal yourself to me. Let the mind and speech enable me to grasp the truth revealed in the *Vedas*. May not my learning forsake me. May I contemplate upon this truth day and night. I think of the truth in mind and I speak of the same. May that *Brahman* protect me. May it protect the teacher. May the *Brahman* protect me. May it protect the teacher. *Om* peace, peace, peace.

ॐ भद्रं नो अपिवातय मनः ।
ॐ शान्तिः शान्तिः शान्तिः ॥८॥

oṃ bhadraṃ no apivātaya manaḥ
oṃ śāntiḥ śāntiḥ śāntiḥ (8)

bhadram - auspiciousness; *naḥ* - for us; *apivātaya* - may you bring about; *manaḥ* - O mind! *oṃ śāntiḥ śāntiḥ śāntiḥ* - *om* peace, peace, peace

O mind! May you make freedom available for us. *Om* peace, peace, peace.

ॐ भद्रं कर्णेभिः शृणुयाम देवाः। भद्रं पश्येमाक्षभिर्यजत्राः।
स्थिरैरङ्गैस्तुष्टुवा सस्तनूभिः। व्यशेम देवहितं यदायुः।
स्वस्ति न इन्द्रो वृद्धश्रवाः। स्वस्ति नः पूषा विश्ववेदाः।
स्वस्ति नस्तार्क्ष्यो अरिष्टनेमिः। स्वस्ति नो बृहस्पतिर्दधातु ।
ॐ शान्तिः शान्तिः शान्तिः॥९॥

oṃ bhadraṃ karṇebhiḥ śruṇuyāma devāḥ / bhadraṃ paśyemākṣabhiryajatrāḥ
sthirairaṅgaistuṣṭuvām̐ sastanūbhiḥ / vyaśemadevahitaṃ yadāyuḥ
svasti na indro vṛddhaśravāḥ / svasti naḥ pūṣā viśvavedāḥ
svasti nastārkṣyo ariṣṭanemiḥ / svasti no bṛhaspatirdadātu
oṃ śāntiḥ śāntiḥ śāntiḥ (9)

bhadram - auspicious; *karṇebhiḥ* - with (our) ears; *śruṇuyāma* - may we listen; *devāḥ* - O gods!; *bhadram* - auspicious; *paśyema* - may we see; *akṣabhiḥ* - with (our) eyes; *yajatrāḥ* - O gods!; *sthiraiḥ* - with strong; *aṅgaiḥ* - limbs; *tuṣṭuvāṃsaḥ* - glorifying (you); *tanūbhiḥ* - through the *Vedas*; *vyaśema* - may we enjoy; *devahitam* - bestowed by the Lord; *yat* - that; *āyuḥ* - (our) full life; *svasti* - auspiciousness; *naḥ* - for us; *indraḥ* - *Indra*; *vṛddhaśravāḥ* - of great fame; (may he bless); *svasti* - auspiciousness; *naḥ* - for us; *pūṣā* - sun deity; *viśvavedāḥ* - the omniscient; *svasti* - auspiciousness; *naḥ* - for us; *tārkṣyaḥ* - *Garuḍa*; *ariṣṭanemiḥ* - of unobstructed flight (may he bless); *svasti* - auspiciousness; *naḥ* - for us; *bṛhaspatiḥ* - *Bṛhaspati*; *dadātu* - may he bless; *oṃ śāntiḥ śāntiḥ śāntiḥ* - *om* peace, peace, peace

O Gods! may we listen to what is meaningful with our ears. May we see with our eyes things that are free from blemish. Glorifying you with Vedic *mantras*, with strong limbs, may we enjoy our full lives. May *Indra* of great fame bless us with auspiciousness. May the omniscient sun deity bless us with auspiciousness. May *Garuḍa* of unobstructed flight bless us with auspiciousness. May *Bṛhaspati* of great intelligence bless us with auspiciousness. *Om* peace, peace, peace.

ॐ यो ब्रह्माणं विदधाति पूर्वं यो वै वेदा श्च प्रहिणोति तस्मै।
त ह देवमात्मबुद्धिप्रकाशं मुमुक्षुर्वै शरणमहं प्रपद्ये॥
ॐ शान्तिः शान्तिः शान्तिः॥ १०॥

oṃ yo brahmāṇāṃ vidadhāti pūrvaṃ yo vai vedām̐śca prahiṇoti tasmai
tam̐ha devamātmabuddhiprakāśaṃ mumukṣurvai śaraṇamahaṃ prapadye
oṃ śāntiḥ śāntiḥ śāntiḥ (10)

yaḥ - he who; *brahmāṇām* - *Brahmā*; *vidadhāti* - creates; *pūrvam* - in the beginning; *yaḥ* - who; *vai* - indeed; *vedān* - *Vedas*; *ca* - and; *prahiṇoti* - taught; *tasmai* - to him; *tam* - that; *ha* - certainly; *devam* - Lord; *ātmabuddhi-prakāśam* - who reveals that self-knowledge; *mumukṣuḥ* - the seeker of freedom; *vai* - indeed; *śaraṇam* - refuge; *aham* - I; *prapadye* - seekṅ *oṃ śāntiḥ śāntiḥ śāntiḥ* - *om* peace, peace, peace

I, a seeker of freedom, seek refuge in that Lord who reveals self-knowledge, who created *Brahmā* in the beginning of creation and who indeed taught him the *Vedas. Om* peace, peace, peace.

Volume III * **Prayers** * Part 10

Ādityahṛdaya Stotram

ततो युद्धपरिश्रान्तं समरे चिन्तया स्थितम् ।
रावणं चाग्रतो दृष्ट्वा युद्धाय समुपस्थितम्॥१॥

tato yuddhapariśrāntaṃ samare cintayā sthitam
rāvaṇaṃ cāgrato dṛṣṭvā yuddhāya samupasthitam (1)

दैवतैश्च समागम्य द्रष्टुमभ्यागतो रणम्।
उपागम्याब्रवीद्रामम् अगस्त्यो भगवानृषिः ॥२॥

daivataiśca samāgamya draṣṭumabhyāgato raṇam
upāgamyābravīdrāmaṃ agastyo bhagavānṛṣiḥ (2)

---

tataḥ - thereafter; *yuddhapariśrāntam* - tired of battle; *samare* - in the battle-field; *cintayā sthitam* - was standing with concern (as to how to kill *Rāvaṇa*); *rāvaṇam* - *Rāvaṇa*; *ca* - and; *agrataḥ* - in front; *dṛṣṭvā* - having seen; *yuddhāya* - for the battle; *samupasthitam* - approaching; *daivataḥ* - with gods; *ca* - and; *samāgamya* - having joined; *draṣṭum* - to see; *abhyāgataḥ* - who came; *raṇam* - battle; *upāgamya* - approaching; *abravīt* - told; *rāmam* - *Rāma*; *agastyaḥ* - *Agastya*; *bhagavān* - *Bhagavān*; *ṛṣiḥ* - sage

Rāma, then, tired of fighting, and seeing *Rāvaṇa* in front, arriving for the war, was standing with concern in the battle-field (as to how to kill *Rāvaṇa*). Approaching that *Rāma*, *Bhagavān* Sage *Agastya*, who came there to see the war surrounded by gods, said these words.

राम राम महाबाहो श्रृणु गुह्यं सनातनम्।
येन सर्वानरीन् वत्स समरे विजयिष्यसि ॥३॥

rāma rāma mahābāho śṛṇu guhyaṃ sanātanam
yena sarvānarīn vatsa samare vijayiṣyasi (3)

rāma - O *Rāma*; *rāma* - O *Rāma*; *mahābāho* - O mighty-armed; *śṛṇu* - listen; *guhyam* - the secret; *sanātanam* - ancient; *yena* - by which; *sarvān* - all; *arīn* - enemies; *vatsa* - O son; *samare* - in the war; *vijayiṣyasi* - you will conquer

O *Rāma*! O son! Listen to this ancient and secret (hymn) by which you will conquer all enemies in the war.

आदित्यं पुण्यं सर्वशत्रुविनाशनम् ।
जयावहं जपेन्नित्यम् आक्षय्यं परमं शिवम् ॥४॥

ādityahṛdayaṃ puṇyaṃ sarvaśatruvināśanam
jayāvahaṃ japennityam akṣayyaṃ paramaṃ śivam (4)

सर्वमङ्गलमाङ्गल्यं सर्व पापप्रणाशनम्।
चिन्ताशोकप्रशमनम् आयुर्वर्धनमुत्तमम् ॥५॥

sarvamaṅgalamāṅgalyaṃ sarvapāpapraṇāśnam
cintāśokapraśamanam āyurvardhanamuttamam (5)

ādityahṛdayaṃ - known as *ādityahṛdaya*; *puṇyaṃ* - purifying; *sarvaśatru-vināśanam* - which destroys all enemies; *jayāvaham* - which brings victory; *japet* - may one chant; *nityam* - always; *akṣayyaṃ* - which has endless result; *paramam* - supreme; *śivam* - auspicious; *sarvamaṅgala-māṅgalyaṃ* - that which is auspicious of all the auspicious prayers; *sarvapāpa-praṇāśnam* - which destroys all *pāpas*; *cintā-śoka-praśamanam* - which eliminates all worries and sorrows; *āyur-vardhanam* - which enhances life-span; *uttamam* - the most exalted prayer

May one chant always this hymn known as *Adityahṛdayam* which is purifying, destroys all enemies, brings victory, has endless result, is the most auspicious, is the auspicious of all the auspicious prayers, destroys all *pāpas*, eliminates all worries and sorrows, enhances the life-span and is the most exalted prayer.

रश्मिमन्तं समुद्यन्तं देवासुरनमस्कृतम् ।
पूजयस्व विवस्वन्तं भास्करं भुवनेश्वरम् ॥६॥

raśmimantaṃ samudyantaṃ devāsuranamaskṛtam
pūjayasva vivasvantaṃ bhāskaram bhuvaneśvaram (6)

raśmimantam - who has rays; *samudyantam* - who is rising; *devāsura-namaskṛtam* - who is saluted by gods and demons; *pūjayasva* - may you worship; *vivasvantam* - the son of *vivasvām*; *bhāskaram* - Lord Sun; *bhuvaneśvaram* - who is the Lord of the universe

May you worship Lord Sun who has (countless) rays, who is rising, who is saluted by gods and demons, the son of *vivasvām* and who is the Lord of the universe.

सर्वदेवात्मको ह्येषः तेजस्वी रश्मिभावनः।
एष देवासुरगणान् लोकान् पाति गभस्तिभि ॥ ७॥

sarvadevātmako hyeṣaḥ tejasvī raśmibhāvanaḥ
eṣa devāsuragaṇān lokān pāti gabhastibhiḥ (7)

sarva-devātmakaḥ - who is the embodiment of all gods; *hi* - indeed; *eṣaḥ* - he; *tejasvī* - brilliant; *raśmibhāvanaḥ* - who creates rays of light; *eṣaḥ* - he; *devāsura-gaṇān* - the host of gods and demons; *lokān* - worlds; *pāti* - protects; *gabhastibhiḥ* - by his bright rays

He is indeed the embodiment of all gods and is brilliant. He creates rays of light. He indeed protects the host of gods and demons, and the worlds by his bright rays.

एष ब्रह्मा च विष्णुश्च शिवस्स्कन्दः प्रजापतिः ।
महेन्द्रो धनदः कालः यमः सोमो ह्यपां पतिः ॥८॥

eṣa brahmā ca viṣṇuśca śivasskandaḥ prajāpatiḥ
mahendro dhanadaḥ kālaḥ yamaḥ somo hyapāṃ patiḥ (8)

eṣaḥ - he; *brahmā* - *Brahmā*; *ca* - and; *viṣṇuḥ* - *Viṣṇu*; *ca* - and; *śivaḥ* - *Śiva*; *skandaḥ* - *Subrahmaṇya*; *prajāpatiḥ* - *Prajāpati*; *mahendraḥ* - the great *Indra*; *dhanadaḥ* - *Kubera* - the giver of wealth; *kālaḥ* - time; *yamaḥ* - *Yama*, deity of death; *somaḥ* - the moon deity; *hi* - indeed; *apām* - of waters; *patiḥ* - Lord (Lord *Varuṇa*)

He is indeed *Brahmā, Viṣṇu, Śiva, Subrahmaṇya, Prajāpati*, Great *Indra, Kubera* - the giver of wealth, the time, *Yama*, the deity of death, the moon deity and indeed the deity of waters (*Varuṇa*).

पितरो वसवः साध्याः ह्यश्विनौ मरुतो मनुः ।
वायुर्वह्निः प्रजाः प्राणः ऋतुकर्त्ता प्रभाकरः ॥९॥

pitaro vasavaḥ sādhyāḥ hyaśvinau maruto manuḥ
vāyurvahniḥ prajāḥ prāṇaḥ ṛtukarttā prabhākaraḥ (9)

pitaraḥ - manes; *vasavaḥ* - the eight deities known as *vasus*; *sādhyāḥ*- the deities known as *sādhyās*; *hi* - indeed; *aśvinau* - *Aśvinikumāras* - the two heavenly physicians; *marutaḥ* - the group of forty-nine deities known as *Maruts*; *manuḥ* - *Manu*; *vāyuḥ* - wind deity; *vahniḥ* - fire deity; *prajāḥ* - the *jīvas*; *prāṇaḥ* - the life-force; *ṛtukarttā* - the cause of seasons; *prabhākaraḥ* - the giver of light

He is indeed the manes, the eight deities known as *Vasus*, the deities known as *Sādhyās*, *Aśvinikumāras*, the two heavenly physicians, the group of forty-nine deities known as *Maruts*, *Manu*, the deity of wind, the deity of fire, the *jīvas*, the life-force, the cause of seasons and the giver of light.

आदित्यस्सविता सूर्यः खगः पूषा गभस्तिमान् ।
सुवर्णसदृशो भानुः हिरण्यरेता दिवाकरः ॥१०॥

ādityassavitā sūryaḥ khagaḥ pūṣā gabhastimān
suvarṇasadṛśo bhānuḥ hiraṇyaretā divākaraḥ (10)

ādityaḥ - son of *Aditi*; *savitā* - the creator of the world; *sūryaḥ* - Lord Sun; *khagaḥ* - who moves in the sky; *pūṣā* - who nourishes the humanity; *gabhastimān* - who has rays; *suvarṇasadṛśaḥ* - who is of golden hue; *bhānuḥ* - who is shining; *hiraṇyaretā* - who is the seed of this universe in the form of knowledge; *divākaraḥ* - who causes the day

He is the son of *Aditi*, the creator of the world, Lord Sun, who moves in the sky, who nourishes the humanity, who has rays, who is of golden hue, who is shining, who is the seed of this universe in the form of knowledge and who causes the day.

हरिदश्वः सहस्रार्चिः सप्तसप्तिर्मरीचिमान्।
तिमिरोन्मथनः शम्भुः त्वष्टा मार्ताण्ड अम्शुमान् ॥ ११॥

haridaśvaḥ sahasrārciḥ saptasaptirmarīcimān
timironmathanaḥ śambhuḥ tvaṣṭā mārtāṇḍa amśumān (11)

haridaśvaḥ - who has green horses; *sahasrārciḥ* - endowed with thousands of rays; *saptasaptiḥ* - who has seven horses; *marīcimān* - who has bright rays; *timironmathanaḥ* - who destroys the darkness; *śambhuḥ* - who causes happiness; *tvaṣṭā* - who dissolves the world; *mārtāṇḍaḥ* - who brings back the dissolved world; *amśumān* - who has all pervasive rays

He is the one who has green horses, who is endowed with thousands of rays, who has seven horses (all the colours of the spectrum), who has bright rays, who destroys the darkness, who causes happiness, who dissolves the world, who brings back the dissolved world and who has all pervasive rays.

हिरण्यगर्भः शिशिरः तपनो भास्करो रविः।
अग्निगर्भोऽदितेः पुत्रः शङ्खश्शिशिरनाशनः॥१२॥

hiraṇyagarbhaḥ śiśiraḥ tapano bhāskaro raviḥ
agnigarbho'diteḥ putraḥ śaṅkhaśśiśiranāśanaḥ (12)

hiraṇyagarbhaḥ - who is Lord in his total manifestation; *śiśiraḥ* - who pleases the mind of the devotees; *tapanaḥ* - who has heat; *bhāskaraḥ* - who is illuminator of everything; *raviḥ* - who is praised by all; *agnigarbhaḥ* - who has fire within himself; *aditeḥ* - of *Aditi*; *putraḥ* - is son; *śaṅkhaḥ* - who sets in the evening; *śiśira-nāśanaḥ* - who destroys morning dew

He is the Lord in his total manifestation, who pleases the mind of the devotees, who has heat, who is illuminator of everything, who is praised by all, who has fire within himself, who is the son of *Aditi*, who sets in the evening and who destroys the morning dew.

व्योमनाथस्तमोभेदी ऋग्यजुस्सामपारगः।
घनवृष्टिरपां मित्रः विन्ध्यवीथीप्लवङ्गमः ॥१३॥

vyomanāthastamobhedī ṛgyajussāmapāragaḥ
ghanavṛṣṭirapāṃ mitraḥ vindhyavīthīplavaṅgamaḥ (13)

vyomanāthaḥ - the Lord of the sky; *tamobhedī* - the destroyer of darkness of ignorance; *ṛg-yajus-sāmapāragaḥ* - who has mastered the three *Vedas, Ṛg, Yajus* and *Sāma*; *ghanavṛṣṭiḥ* - who causes heavy rains; *apāṃ* - of waters; *mitraḥ* - is friend; *vindhyavīthī-plavaṅgamaḥ* - who moves about through the Vindhya Mountains in the Southern Solstice

He is the Lord of sky, the destroyer of darkness of ignorance, the one who has mastered the three *Vedas, Ṛg, Yajus* and *Sāma*, causes heavy rains, who is friend of waters, moves about through the Vindhya Mountains in the Southern Solstice.

आतपी मण्डली मृत्युः पिङ्गलस्सर्वतापनः ।
कविर्विश्वो महातेजाः रक्तस्सर्वभवोद्भवः ॥१४॥

ātapī maṇḍalī mṛtyuḥ piṅgalassarvatāpanaḥ
kavirviśvo mahātejāḥ raktassarvabhavodbhavaḥ (14)

ātapī - who is the daylight; *maṇḍalī* - who has circular shape; *mṛtyuḥ* - who is death; *piṅgalaḥ* - who has golden hue; *sarvatāpanaḥ* - who scorches all; *kaviḥ* - who is omniscient; *viśvaḥ* - who is all forms; *mahātejāḥ* - who has great brilliance; *raktaḥ* - who is all love; *sarvabhavodbhavaḥ* - who is the cause of all births

He is one who is the daylight, who has circular shape, who is death himself, who has golden hue, who scorches all, who is omniscient, who is all forms, who has great brilliance, who ia all love and who is the cause of all births.

नक्षत्रग्रहताराणाम् अधिपो विश्वभावनः।
तेजसामपि तेजस्वी द्वादशात्मन् नमोऽस्तुते॥१५॥

nakṣatragrahatārāṇām adhipo viśvabhāvanaḥ
tejasāmapi tejasvī dvādaśātman namo'stu te (15)

nakṣatra-graha-tārāṇām - of stars, planets and other luminaries; *adhipaḥ* - the presiding deity; *viśvabhāvanaḥ* - who is the protector of the universe; *tejasām* - of all lights ones; *api* - even; *tejasvī* - the light; *dvādaśātman* - O one who has twelve forms; *namaḥ* - salutation; *astu* - let it be; *te* - unto you

He is the one who is the presiding deity of stars, planets and other luminaries, who is the protector of the universe and who is the light of all lights. O one who has twelve forms! Let (my) salutations be unto you.

नमः पूर्वाय गिरये पश्चिमायाद्रये नमः।
ज्योतिर्गणानां पतये दिनाधिपतये नमः ॥१६॥

namaḥ pūrvāya giraye paścimāyādraye namaḥ
jyotirgaṇānāṃ pataye dinādhipataye namaḥ (16)

namaḥ - salutation; *pūrvāya giraye* - to the one who has the eastern mountain for his rise; *paścimāya adraye* - to the one who has the western mountain as his setting place; *namaḥ* - salutation; *jyotirgaṇānāṃ* - of the groups of luminaries; *pataye* - to the Lord; *dinādhipataye* - to the one who is the Lord of the day; *namaḥ* - salutation

Salutation to the one who has the eastern mountain for his rise and the western mountain as his setting place. Salutation to the Lord of the groups of luminaries, and salutation to the one who is the Lord of the day.

जयाय जयभद्राय हर्यश्वाय नमो नमः ।
नमो नमः सहस्रांशः आदित्याय नमो नमः ॥ १७॥

jayāya jayabhadrāya haryaśvāya namo namaḥ
namo namaḥ sahasrāṃśaḥ ādityāya namo namaḥ (17)

jayāya - to the victorious; *jayabhadrāya* - to the giver of victory and prosperity; *haryaśvāya* - to the one who has green horse; *namaḥ namaḥ* - repeated salutations; *namaḥ namaḥ* - repeated salutations; *sahasrāṃśaḥ* - one who has thousands of rays; *ādityāya* - to the son of *Aditi*; *namaḥ namaḥ* - repeated salutations

Repeated salutations to the victorious and the giver of victory and prosperity. Repeated salutations to the one who has green horse, who has thousands of rays and who is the son of *Aditi*.

नम उग्राय वीराय सारङ्गाय नमो नमः।
नमः पद्मप्रबोधाय मार्ताण्डाय नमो नमः॥ १८॥

nama ugrāya vīryāya sāraṅgāya namo namaḥ
namaḥ padmaprabodhāya mārtāṇḍāya namo namaḥ (18)

namaḥ - salutation; *ugrāya* - to the one who is fierce-looking (towards the unrighteous); *vīryāya* - who has valour; *sāraṅgāya* - who is a fast mover; *namaḥ namaḥ* - repeated salutations; *namaḥ* - salutation; *padma-prabodhāya* - who makes the lotus blossom; *mārtāṇḍāya* - who is the prime cause; *namaḥ namaḥ* - repeated salutations

Repeated salutations to the one who is fierce-looking (towards unrighteous), who has valour, who is a fast mover, who makes the lotus blossom and who is the prime cause.

ब्रह्मेशानाच्युतेशाय सूर्यायादित्यवर्चसे ।
भास्वते सर्वभक्षाय रौद्राय वपुषे नमः ॥ १९॥

brahmeśānācyuteśāya sūryāyādityavarcase
bhāsvate sarvabhakṣāya raudrāya vapuṣe namaḥ (19)

brahmā-īśāna-acyuta-īśāya - to the Lord of *Brahmā, Śiva* and *Viṣṇu*; *sūryāya* - to Lord Sun; *ādityavarcase* - to the light of Sun; *bhāsvate* - to the shining one; *sarvabhakṣāya* - to the one who devours everything; *raudrāya vapuṣe* - to the one whose form is fierce; *namaḥ* - salutation

Salutation to the Lord of *Brahmā, Śiva* and *Viṣṇu,* who is Lord Sun, who is the light of Sun, who is the shining one, who devours everything and whose form is fierce.

तमोघ्नाय हिमघ्नाय शत्रुघ्नायामितात्मने ।
कृतघ्नघ्नाय देवाय ज्योतिषां पतये नमः ॥ २० ॥

tamoghnāya himaghnāya śatrughnāyāmitātmane
kṛtaghnaghnāya devāya jyotiṣāṃ pataye namaḥ (20)

tamoghnāya - to the one who removes the darkness; *himaghnāya* - to the one who removes fog; *śatrughnāya* - to the one who destroys the enemies; *āmitātmane* - to the one who is limitless; *kṛtaghnaghnāya* - to the one who destroys the ungrateful; *devāya* - to the shining one; *jyotiṣāṃ* - of the luminaries; *pataye* - to the Lord; *namaḥ* - salutation

Salutation to the one who removes the darkness, who removes fog, who destroys the enemies, who is limitless, who destroys the ungrateful, who is the shining one and who is the Lord of the luminaries.

तप्तचामीकराभाय वह्नये विश्वकर्मणे।
नमस्तमोऽभिनिघ्नाय रुचये लोकसाक्षिणे ॥ २१ ॥

taptacāmīkarābhāya vahnaye viśvakarmaṇe
namastamo'bhinighnāya rucaye lokasākṣiṇe (21)

taptacāmīkarābhāya - to the one who has the complexion of molten gold; *vahnaye* - to the one who is of the nature of fire; *viśvakarmaṇe* - to the one whose action is of creating the world; *namaḥ* - salutation; *tamo'bhinighnāya* - to the one who removes the darkness of ignorance; *rucaye* - to the one who is shining; *lokasākṣiṇe* - to the one who is the witness of the world

Salutation to the one who has the complexion of molten gold, who is of the nature of fire, whose action is of creating the world, who removes the darkness of ignorance, who is shining, and who is the witness of the world.

नाशयत्येष वै भूतं तदेव सृजति प्रभुः।
पायत्येषः तपत्येषः वर्षत्येष गभस्तिभिः ॥ २२ ॥

nāśayatyeṣa vai bhūtaṃ tadeva sṛjati prabhuḥ
pāyatyeṣaḥ tapatyeṣaḥ varṣatyeṣa gabhastibhiḥ (22)

nāśayati - destroys; *eṣaḥ* - he; *vai* - indeed; *bhūtam* - beings; *tadeva* - that alone; *sṛjati* - creates; *prabhuḥ* - the Lord; *pāyati* - dries up everything; *eṣaḥ* - he; *tapati* - scorches; *eṣaḥ* - he; *varṣati* - pours as rains; *eṣaḥ* - he; *gabhastibhiḥ* - through the rays

He, the Lord, indeed destroys beings and creates them alone. He dries up everything, scorches and pours as rains, through the rays.

एष सुप्तेषु जागर्त्ति भूतेषु परिनिष्ठतः ।
एष एवाग्निहोत्रं च फलं चैवाग्निहोत्रिणाम् ॥२३॥

eṣa supteṣu jāgartti bhūteṣu pariniṣṭhitaḥ
eṣa evāgnihotraṃ ca phalaṃ caivāgnihotriṇām (23)

eṣaḥ - he; *supteṣu* - while sleeping; *jāgartti* - keeps awake; *bhūteṣu* - in beings; *pariniṣṭhitaḥ*- abiding; *eṣaḥ* - he; *eva* - alone; *agnihotram* - is the ritual called *agnihotra*; *ca* - and; *phalam* - result; *ca* - also; *evā* - indeed; *agnihotriṇām* - for those who do *agnihotra*

He abiding in the beings, keeps awake, while they are asleep. He alone is the ritual called *agnihotra* and also the result for those who do *agnihotra*.

वेदाश्च क्रतवश्चैव क्रतूनां फलमेव च ।
यानि कृत्यानि लोकेषु सर्व एष रविः प्रभुः ॥२४॥

vedāśca kratavaścaiva kratūnāṃ phalameva ca
yāni kṛtyāni lokeṣu sarva eṣa raviḥ prabhuḥ (24)

vedāḥ - *Vedās*; *ca* - and; *kratavaḥ* - fire rituals; *ca* - and; *eva* - indeed; *kratūnām* - of the fire rituals; *phalam* - result; *eva* - indeed; *ca* - and; *yāni* - whatever; *kṛtyāni* - duties; *lokeṣu* - in the worlds; *sarvaḥ* - all; *eṣaḥ* - he; *raviḥ* - Lord Sun; *prabhuḥ* - the Lord

He indeed is the *Vedās*, fire rituals, the result of the fire rituals, and also whatever duties are there in the worlds, all that is Lord Sun, the Lord alone.

एनमापत्सु कृच्छ्रेषु कान्तारेषु भयेषु च ।
कीर्तयन् पुरुषः कश्चित् नावसीदति राघव ॥ २५॥

enamāpatsu kṛcchreṣu kāntāreṣu bhayeṣu ca
kīrtayan puruṣaḥ kaścit nāvasīdati rāghava (25)

enam - this (stotram); *āpatsu* - in times of danger; *kṛcchreṣu* - in times of afflictions like fever; *kāntāreṣu* - in the forest; *bhayeṣu* - when there is fear; *ca* - and; *kīrtayan* - chanting; *puruṣaḥ* - a person; *kaścit* - anyone; *na* - not; *avasīdati* - come to grief; *rāghava* - O *Rāma*

Chanting this stotram in times of danger, in times of afflictions like fever, in the forest and when there is fear, any person does not come to grief, O *Rāma*.

पूजयस्वैनमेकाग्रः देवदेवं जगत्पतिम् ।
एतत् त्रिगुणितं जप्त्वा युद्धेषु विजयिष्यसि ॥२६॥

pūjayasvainamekāgraḥ devadevaṃ jagatpatim
etat triguṇitaṃ japtvā yuddheṣu vijayiṣyasi (26)

pūjayasva - may you worship; *enam* - him; *ekāgraḥ* - with single-pointedness; *devadevam* - the Lord of gods; *jagatpatim* - the Lord of the universe; *etat* - this; *triguṇitam* - three times; *japtvā* - chanting; *yuddheṣu* - in the wars; *vijayiṣyasi* - you will achieve victory

May you worship this Lord of the deities, the Lord of the universe with single-pointedness, chanting this *stotra* three times in the wars you will achieve victory.

अस्मिन् क्षणे महाबाहो रावणं त्वं वधिष्यसि।
एवमुक्त्वा तदागस्त्यः जगाम च यथागतम् ॥२७॥

asmin kṣaṇe mahābhāho rāvaṇaṃ tvaṃ vadhiṣyasi
evamuktvā tadāgastyaḥ jagāma ca yathāgatam (27)

asmin - in this; *kṣaṇe* - moment; *mahābhāho* - O mighty armed; *rāvaṇam* - *Rāvaṇa*; *tvam* - you; *vadhiṣyasi* - will kill; *evam* - thus; *uktvā* - having said; *tadā* - then; *agastyaḥ* - Sage *Agastya*; *jagāma* - went away; *ca* - and; *yathāgatam* - the way he came

At this moment, O mighty armed, you will kill *Rāvaṇa*. And having said thus, Sage *Agastya* went away the way he came.

एतच्छ्रुत्वा महातेजाः नष्टशोकोऽभवत्तदा ।
धारयामास सुप्रीतः राघवः प्रयतात्मवान् ॥२८॥

etacchrutvā mahātejāḥ naṣṭaśoko'bhavattadā
dhārayāmāsa suprītaḥ rāghavaḥ prayatātmavān (28)

etat - this; *śrutvā* - having heard; *mahātejāḥ* - the great brilliant one; *naṣṭaśokaḥ* - free from sorrow; *abhavat* - became; *tadā* - then; *dhārayāmāsa* - meditated upon Lord Sun; *suprītaḥ* - with pleased disposition; *rāghavaḥ* - *Rāma*; *prayatātmavān* - with disciplined mind

Having heard this, *RṬma*, the great brilliant one, became free from sorrow. Then, with pleased disposition and disciplined mind, he meditated upon Lord Sun.

आदित्यं प्रेक्ष्य जप्त्वा तु परं हर्षमवाप्तवान् ।
त्रिराचम्य शुचिर्भूत्वा धनुरादाय वीर्यवान् ॥२९॥

ādityaṃ prekṣya japtvā tu paraṃ harṣamavāptavān
trirācamya śucirbhūtvā dhanurādhāya vīryavān (29)

ādityam - Lord Sun; *prekṣya* - seeing; *japtvā* - having chanted; *tu* - indeed; *param* - great; *harṣam* - happiness; *avāptavān* - gained; *triḥ* - three times; *ācamya* - sipping water ceremoniously; *śuciḥ-bhūtvā* - having become pure; *dhanuḥ* - bow; *ādhāya* - taking; *vīryavān* - one who is valorous

After sipping water ceremoniously three times and indeed having become pure, he who has valour, having seen Lord Sun and having chanted, taking the bow in his hands, gained great happiness.

रावणं प्रक्ष्य हृष्टात्मा युद्धाय समुपागतम्।
सर्वयत्नेन महता वधे तस्य धृतोऽभवत् ॥३०॥

rāvaṇaṃ prekṣya hṛṣṭātmā yuddhāya samupāgatam
sarvayatnena mahātā vadhe tasya dhṛto'bhavat (30)

rāvaṇam - *Rāvaṇa*; *prekṣya* - seeing; *hṛṣṭātmā* - one who is pleased; *yuddhāya* - for the battle; *samupāgatam* - who has come prepared; *sarvayatnena* - with all effort; *mahātā* - great; *vadhe* - in killing; *tasya* - of him; *dhṛtaḥ abhavat* - became resolved

Being pleased at seeing *Rāvaṇa* who has come prepared for the battle, he became resolved in killing him with all great efforts.

अथ रविरवदन्निरीक्ष्य रामं
मुदितमनाः परमं प्रहृष्यमाणः।
निशिचरपति संक्षयं विदित्वा
सुरगणमध्यगतो वचस्त्वरेति ॥ ३२॥

atha raviravadannirīkṣya rāmaṃ
muditamanāḥ paramaṃ prahṛṣyamāṇaḥ
niśicarapatisaṃkṣayaṃ viditvā
suragaṇamadhyagato vacastvareti (31)

atha - then; *raviḥ* - Lord Sun; *avadat* - told; *nirīkṣya* - seeing; *rāmam* - *Rāma*; *muditamanāḥ* - with a pleased mind; *paramam* - great; *prahṛṣyamāṇaḥ* - being elated; *niśicarapati* - *saṃkṣayam* - the destruction of the king of the demons; *viditvā* - knowing; *suragaṇamadhyagataḥ* - abiding in the midst of the host of *devas*; *vacaḥ* - words; *tvara* - hurry up; *iti* - thus

Then, Lord Sun, with a pleased mind, seeing *Rāma* and being greatly elated, knew the imminent estruction of the king of the demons, and abiding in the midst of the host of *devas* said the words, "hurry up".

Śrī Annapūrṇā Stotram

नित्यानन्दकरी वराभयकरी सौन्दर्यरत्नाकरी
निर्धूताखिलघोरपापनिकरी प्रत्यक्षमाहेश्वरी ।
प्रालेयाचलवंशपावनकरी काशीपुराधीश्वरी
भिक्षां देहि कृपावलम्बनकरी मातान्नपूर्णेश्वरी ॥१॥

nityānandakarī varābhayakarī saundaryaratnākarī
nirdhūtākhilaghorapāpanikarī pratyakṣamāheśvarī
prāleyācalavaṃśapāvanakarī kāśīpurādhīśvarī
bhikṣāṃ dehi kṛpāvalambanakarī mātānnapūrṇeśvarī (1)

nityānandakarī - one who gives permanent happiness; *varābhayakarī* - one whose hands grant boons and fearlessness; *saundaryaratnākarī* - one who is ocean of beauty; *nirdhūtākhila-ghorapāpanikarī* - one who destroys all the terrifying sins; *pratyakṣamāheśvarī* - one who herself is the supreme Goddess; *prāleyācalavaṃśa-pāvanakarī*- one who purifies the lineage of Mount *Himavān*; *kāśīpurādhīśvarī* - one who is the presiding deity of the city of *Vārāṇasī*; *bhikṣām* - food; *dehi* - may you give; *kṛpāvalambanakarī* - one who gives the support of her grace; *mātā* - one who is mother (of the universe); *annapūrṇeśvarī* - one who is Goddess *Annapūrṇā*

May you, Goddess *Annapūrṇā*, who gives permanent happiness, whose hands grant boons and fearlessness, who is the ocean of beauty, who destroys all terrifiying sins, who herself is the supreme Goddess, who purifies the lineage of Mount *Himavān*, who is the presiding deity of the city of *Vārāṇasī*, who gives the support of her grace and who is the mother (of the universe), give *bhikṣā*, food.

नानारत्नविचित्रभूषणकरी हेमाम्बराडम्बरी
मुक्ताहारविलम्बमानविलसद्वक्षोजकुम्भान्तरी ।
काश्मीरागरुवासिता रुचिकरी काशीपुराधीश्वरी
भिक्षां देहि कृपावलम्बनकरी मातान्नपूर्णेश्वरी ॥२॥

nānāratnavicitrabhūṣaṇakarī hemāmbarāḍambarī
muktāhāravilambamānavilasadvakṣojakumbhāntarī
kāśmīrāgaruvāsitā rucikarī kāśīpurādhīśvarī
bhikṣāṃ dehi kṛpāvalambanakarī mātānnapūrṇeśvarī (2)

nānāratnavicitrabhūṣaṇakarī - one who has many unique ornaments made of gem in her hand; *hemāmbarāḍambarī* - one who is adorned with yellow cloth; *muktāhāra-vilambamāna-vilasadvakṣoja-kumbhāntarī* - one whose chest has pot-like breasts adorned with hanging pearl necklaces; *kāśmīrāgaruvāsitā* - one who is made fragrant by the incence of *Kāśmīra*; *rucikarī* - one who gives beauty; *kāśīpurādhīśvarī* - one who is the presiding deity of the city of *Vārāṇasī*; *bhikṣām* - food; *dehi* - may you give; *kṛpāvalambanakarī* - one who gives the support of her grace; *mātā* - one who is mother (of the universe); *annapūrṇeśvarī* - one who is Goddess *Annapūrṇā*

May you, Goddess *Annapūrṇā*, who has many unique ornaments made of gem in her hand, who is adorned with yellow cloth, whose chest has pot-like breasts adorned with hanging pearl necklaces, who is made fragrant by the incence of *Kāśmīra*, who gives beauty, who is the presiding deity of the city of *Vārāṇasī*, who gives the support of her grace and who is the mother (of the universe), give *bhikṣā*, food.

योगानन्दकरी रिपुक्षयकरी धर्मैकनिष्ठाकरी
चन्द्रार्कनलभासमानलहरी त्रैलोक्यरक्षाकरी ।
सर्वैश्वर्यकरी तपःफलकरी काशीपुराधीश्वरी
भिक्षां देहि कृपावलम्बनकरी मातान्नपूर्णेश्वरी ॥३॥

yogānandakarī ripukṣayakarī dharmaikaniṣṭhākarī
candrārkānalabhāsamānalaharī trailokyarakṣākarī
sarvaiśvaryakarī tapaḥphalakarī kāśīpurādhīśvarī
bhikṣāṃ dehi kṛpāvalambanakarī mātānnapūrṇeśvarī (3)

yogānandakarī - one who gives happiness of eightfold *yoga*; *ripukṣayakarī*- one who destroys enemies; *dharmaikaniṣṭhākarī* - one who is solely commited to *dharma*; *candrārkānala-bhāsamānalaharī* - one who has the shine equal to that of moon, sun and fire; *trailokyarakṣākarī* - one who is the protector of the three worlds; *sarvaiśvaryakarī* - one who grants all prosperities; *tapaḥphalakarī* - one who gives the fruits of austerities; *kāśīpurādhīśvarī* - one who is the presiding deity of the city of *Vārāṇasī*; *bhikṣām* - food; *dehi* - may you give; *kṛpāvalambanakarī* - one who gives the support of her grace; *mātā* - one who is mother (of the universe); *annapūrṇeśvarī* - one who is Goddess *Annapūrṇā*

May you, Goddess *Annapūrṇā*, who gives happiness of eightfold *yoga*, who destroys enemies, who is solely commited to *dharma*, who has the shine equal to that of moon, sun and fire, who is the protector of the three worlds, who grants all prosperities, who gives the fruits of austerities, who is the presiding deity of the city of *Vārāṇasī*, who gives the support of her grace and who is the mother (of the universe), give *bhikṣā*, food.

कैलासाचलकन्दरालयकरी गौरी ह्युमा शाङ्करी
कौमारी निगमार्थगोचरकरीह्योङ्कारबीजाक्षरी।
मोक्षद्वारकवाटपाटनकरी काशीपुराधीश्वरी
भिक्षां देहि कृपावलम्बनकरी मातान्नपूर्णेश्वरी ॥४॥

kailāsācalakandarālayakarī gaurī hyumā śāṅkarī
kaumārī nigamārthagocarakarī hyoṅkārabījākṣarī
mokṣadvārakavāṭapāṭanakarī kāśīpurādhīśvarī
bhikṣāṃ dehi kṛpāvalambanakarī mātānnapūrṇeśvarī (4)

kailāsācalakandarālayakarī - one who has the cave of *Kailāsā* mountain as her abode; *gaurī* - one who is white-complexioned; *hi umā* - one who is indeed *Umā*; *śāṅkarī* - one who is the consort of Lord *Śiva*; *kaumārī* - one who is always endowed with youth; *nigamārthagocarakarī* - one who makes others know the meaning of *Vedas*; *hi oṅkāra-bījākṣarī* - one who has *om* as the basic syllable; *mokṣadvārakavāṭapāṭanakarī* - one who opens the door of the heaven; *kāśīpurādhīśvarī* - one who is the presiding deity of the city of *Vārāṇasī*; *bhikṣām* - food; *dehi* - may you give; *kṛpāvalambanakarī* - one who gives the support of her grace; *mātā* - one who is mother (of the universe); *annapūrṇeśvarī* - one who is Goddess *Annapūrṇā*

May you, Goddess *Annapūrṇā*, who has the cave of *Kailāsā* mountain as her abode, who is white-complexioned, who is *Umā*, who is the consort of Lord *Śiva*, who is always endowed with youth, who makes others know the meaning of *Vedas*, who has *Om* as the basic syllable, who opens the door of the heaven, who is the presiding deity of the city of *Vārāṇasī*, who gives the support of her grace and who is the mother (of the universe), give *bhikṣā*, food.

दृश्यादृश्यविभूतिवाहनकरी ब्रह्माण्डभाण्डोदरी
लीलानाटकसूत्रखेलनकरी विज्ञानदीपाङ्कुरी ।
श्रीविश्वेशमनःप्रसादनकरी काशीपुराधीश्वरी
भिक्षां देहि कृपावलम्बनकरी मातान्नपूर्णेश्वरी ॥५॥

dṛśyādṛśyavibhūtivāhanakarī brahmāṇḍabhāṇḍodarī
līlānāṭakasūtrakhelanakarī vijñānadīpāṅkurī
śrīviśveśamanaḥprasādanakarī kāśīpurādhīśvarī
bhikṣāṃ dehi kṛpāvalambanakarī mātānnapūrṇeśvarī (5)

dṛśyādṛśyavibhūtivāhanakarī - one who is the cause of the spread of glories of gross and subtle universe; *brahmāṇḍabhāṇḍodarī* - one who wields the vessel of universe in her stomach; *līlānāṭakasūtrakhelanakarī* - one who playfully wields the reins of puppet show of the world; *vijñānadīpāṅkurī* - one who is the light of the lamp of knowledge; *śrīviśveśamanaḥ-prasādanakarī* - one who gives happiness to the mind of Lord *Śiva*; *kāśīpurādhīśvarī* - one who is the presiding deity of the city of *Vārāṇasī*; *bhikṣām* - food; *dehi* - may you give; *kṛpāvalambanakarī* - one who gives the support of her grace; *mātā* - one who is mother (of the universe); *annapūrṇeśvarī* - one who is Goddess *Annapūrṇā*

May you, Goddess *Annapūrṇā*, who is the cause of the spread of glories of gross and subtle universe, who wields the vessel of universe in her stomach, who playfully wields the reins of puppet show of the world, who is the light of the lamp of knowledge, who gives happiness to the mind of Lord *Śiva*, who is the presiding deity of the city of *Vārāṇasī*, who gives the support of her grace and who is the mother (of the universe), give *bhikṣā*, food.

उर्वी सर्वजनेश्वरी जयकरी माता कृपासागरी
वेणीनीलसमानकुन्तलधरी नित्यान्नदानेश्वरी ।
साक्षान्मोक्षकरी सदा शुभकरी काशीपुराधीश्वरी
भिक्षां देहि कृपावलम्बनकरी मातान्नपूर्णेश्वरी ॥६॥

urvī sarvajaneśvarī jayakarī matā kṛpāsāgarī
veṇīnīlasamānakuntaladharī nityānnadāneśvarī
sākṣānmokṣakarī sadā śubhakarī kāśīpurādhīśvarī
bhikṣāṃ dehi kṛpāvalambanakarī mātānnapūrṇeśvarī (6)

urvī - one who is in the form of earth; *sarvajaneśvarī* - one who is the Goddess of all; *jayakarī* - one who gives success; *matā* - one who is the mother (of the universe); *kṛpāsāgarī* - one who is the ocean of compassion; *veṇīnīlasamānakuntaladharī*- one who is dressed with beautiful braided black hair; *nityānnadāneśvarī* - one who daily does charity of food; *sākṣānmokṣakarī* - one who gives freedom herself; *sadā śubhakarī*- one who always gives good; *kāśīpurādhīśvarī*- one who is the presiding deity of the city of *Vārāṇasī*; *bhikṣām* - food; *dehi* - may you give; *kṛpāvalambanakarī* - one who gives the support of her grace; *mātā* - one who is mother (of the universe); *annapūrṇeśvarī* - one who is Goddess *Annapūrṇā*

May you, Goddess *Annapūrṇā*, who is in the form of earth, who is the Goddess of all who gives success, who is the mother (of the universe), who is the ocean of compassion, who is dressed with beautiful braided hair, whose hair is black, who daily does charity of food, who gives freedom herself, who always gives good, who is the presiding deity of the city of *Vārāṇasī*, who gives the support of her grace and who is the mother (of the universe), give *bhikṣā*, food.

आदिक्षान्तसमस्तवर्णनकरी शम्भोस्त्रिभावाकरी
काश्मीरा त्रिपुरेश्वरी त्रिणयनी विश्वेश्वरी शर्वरी ।
स्वर्गद्वारकवाटपाटनकरी काशीपुराधीश्वरी
भिक्षां देहि कृपावलम्बनकरी मातान्नपूर्णेश्वरी ॥७॥

ādikṣāntasamastavarṇanakarī śambhostribhāvākarī
kāśmīrā tripureśvarī triṇayanī viśveśvarī śarvarī
svargadvārakavāṭapāṭanakarī kāśīpurādhīśvarī
bhikṣāṃ dehi kṛpāvalambanakarī mātānnapūrṇeśvarī (7)

ādikṣāntasamastavarṇanakarī - one who is the author of all syllables from *a* to *kṣa*; *śambhoḥ* - of Lord *Śiva*; *tribhāvākarī* - one who is the abode of the three functions viz. creation, sustenance and dissolution; *kāśmīrā* - one who wears *kunkuma*, vermilion; *tripureśvarī* - one who is the Goddess of three cities (of waking, dream and sleep); *triṇayanī* - one who is the consort of three eyed Lord; *viśveśvarī* - one who is the Goddess of the universe; *śarvarī* - one who is the deity of night; *svargadvārakavāṭapāṭanakarī* - one who opens the door to the heaven; *kāśīpurādhīśvarī* - one who is the presiding deity of the city of *Vārāṇasī*; *bhikṣām* - food; *dehi* - may you give; *kṛpāvalambanakarī* - one who gives the support of her grace; *mātā* - one who is mother (of the universe); *annapūrṇeśvarī* - one who is Goddess *Annapūrṇā*

May you, Goddess *Annapūrṇā*, who is the author of all syllables from *a* to *kṣa*, who is the abode of the three functions of the Lord viz. creation, sustenance and dissolution, who wears *kuṅkuma*, vermilion, who is the Goddess of three cities (of waking, dream, and sleep),who is the consort of the three eyed Lord, who is the Goddess of the universe, who is the deity of night, who opens the door to the heaven, who is the presiding deity of the city of *Vārāṇasī*, who gives the support of her grace and who is the mother (of the universe), give *bhikṣā*, food.

देवी सर्वविचित्ररत्नरचिता दाक्षायणी सुन्दरी
वामा स्वादुपयोधरा प्रियकरी सौभाग्यमाहेश्वरी ।
भक्ताभीष्टकरी सदा शुभकरी काशीपुराधीश्वरी
भिक्षां देहि कृपावलम्बनकरी मातान्नपूर्णेश्वरी ।। ८ ।।

devī sarvavicitraratnaracitā dākṣāyaṇī sundarī
vāmā svādupayodharā priyakarī saubhāgyamāheśvarī
bhaktābhīṣṭakarī sadā śubhakarī kāśīpurādhīśvarī
bhikṣāṃ dehi kṛpāvalambanakarī mātānnapūrṇeśvarī (8)

devī - one who is shining; *sarvavicitraratnaracitā* - one who is decorated with all variegated gems; *dākṣāyaṇī* - one who is the daughter of *Daksa*, a *prajāpati*; *sundarī* - one who is a beautiful woman; *vāmā svādupayodharā* - one who has beautiful breasts; *priyakarī* - one who does pleasing things; *saubhāgyamāheśvarī* - one who is the consort of Lord *Śiva* and endowed with all fortunes; *bhaktābhīṣṭakarī* - one who grants the desired things to the devotees; *sadā śubhakarī* - one who is always doing good; *kāśīpurādhīśvarī* - one who is the presiding deity of the city of *Vārāṇasī*; *bhikṣām* - food; *dehi* - may you give; *kṛpāvalambanakarī* - one who gives the support of her grace; *mātā* - one who is mother (of the universe); *annapūrṇeśvarī* - one who is Goddess *Annapūrṇā*

May you, Goddess *Annapūrṇā*, who is shining, who is decorated with all variegated gems, who is the daughter of *Dakṣa*, a *prajāpati*, who is a beautiful woman, who has beautiful breasts, who does pleasing things, who is the consort of Lord *Śiva* and endowed with all fortunes, who grants the desired things to the devotees, who is always doing good, who is the presiding deity of the city of *Vārāṇasī*, who gives the support of her grace and who is the mother (of the universe), give *bhikṣā*, food.

चन्द्रार्कानलकोटिकोटिसदृशी चन्द्रांशुबिम्बाधरी
चन्द्रार्काग्निसमानकुण्डलधरी चन्द्रार्कवर्णेश्वरी ।
मालापुस्तकपाशसाङ्कुशधरी काशीपुराधीश्वरी
भिक्षां देहि कृपावलम्बनकरी मातान्नपूर्णेश्वरी ॥ ९ ॥

candrārkānalakoṭikoṭisadṛśī candrāṃśubimbādharī
candrārkāgnisamānakuṇḍaladharī candrārkavarṇeśvarī
mālāpustakapāśasāṅkuśadharī kāśīpurādhīśvarī
bhikṣāṃ dehi kṛpāvalambanakarī mātānnapūrṇeśvarī (9)

candrārkānalakoṭikoṭisadṛśī - one who is equal to crores of moon, sun and fire; *candrāṃśu-bimbādharī* - one who has lips like moon-ray and a particular red fruit; *candrārkāgni-samāna-kuṇḍaladharī* - one who wears ear-rings having the shine of moon, sun and fire; *candrārkavarṇeśvarī* - one who has the colour of moon and sun; *mālāpustakapāśasāṅkuśadharī* - one who holds garland, book, noose and goad; *kāśīpurādhīśvarī* - one who is the presiding deity of the city of *Vārāṇasī*; *bhikṣām* - food; *dehi* - may you give; *kṛpāvalambanakarī* - one who gives the support of her grace; *mātā* - one who is mother (of the universe); *annapūrṇeśvarī* - one who is Goddess *Annapūrṇā*

May you, Goddess *Annapūrṇā*, who is equal to countless crores of moon, sun and fire, who has lips like moon-ray and a particular red fruit, who wears ear-rings having the shine of moon, sun and fire, who has the colour of moon and sun, who holds garland, book, noose and goad, who is the presiding deity of the city of *Vārāṇasī*, who gives the support of her grace and who is the mother (of the universe), give *bhikṣā*, food.

क्षत्रत्राणकरी महाभयकरी माता कृपासागरी
सर्वानन्दकरी सदा शिवकरी विश्वेश्वरी श्रीधरी ।
दक्षाक्रन्दकरी निरामयकरी काशीपुराधीश्वरी
भिक्षां देहि कृपावलम्बनकरी मातान्नपूर्णेश्वरी ॥ १० ॥

kṣatratrāṇakarī mahābhayaharī mātā kṛpāsāgarī
sarvānandakarī sadā śivakarī viśveśvarī śrīdharī
dakṣākrandakarī nirāmayakarī kāśīpurādhīśvarī
bhikṣāṃ dehi kṛpāvalambanakarī mātānnapūrṇeśvarī (10)

kṣatratrāṇakarī - one who protects the warrior class; *mahābhayaharī* - one who gives fearlessness and is great; *mātā* - one who is mother (of the universe); *kṛpāsāgarī* - one who is ocean of compassion; *sarvānandakarī* - one who gives happiness to all; *sadā śivakarī* - one who always does good; *viśveśvarī* - one who is the Goddess of universe; *śrīdharī* - one who is in the form of Goddess *Lakṣmī*; *dakṣākrandakarī* - one who made *Dakṣa* cry; *nirāmayakarī* - one who is the remover of all diseases; *kāśīpurādhīśvarī* - one who is the presiding deity of the city of *Vārāṇasī*; *bhikṣām* - food; *dehi* - may you give; *kṛpāvalambanakarī* - one who gives the support of her grace; *mātā* - one who is mother (of the universe); *annapūrṇeśvarī* - one who is Goddess *Annapūrṇā*

May you, Goddess *Annapūrṇā*, who protects the warrior class, who gives fearlessness and is great, who is the mother (of the universe), who is ocean of compassion, who gives happiness to all, who always does good, who is the Goddess of universe, who is in the form of Goddess *Lakṣmī*, who made *Dakṣa* cry, who is the remover of all diseases, who is the presiding deity of the city of *Vārāṇasī*, who gives the support of her grace and who is the mother (of the universe), give *bhikṣā*, food.

अन्नपूर्णे सदा पूर्णे शङ्करप्राणवल्लभे ।
ज्ञानवैराग्यसिद्ध्यर्थं भिक्षां देहि च पार्वती ॥ ११॥

annapūrṇe sadāpūrṇe śaṅkaraprāṇavallabhe
jñānavairāgyasiddhyarthaṃ bhikṣāṃ dehi ca pārvatī (11)

annapūrṇe - O *Annapūrṇā*!; *sadāpūrṇe* - one who is always full; *śaṅkaraprāṇa-vallabhe* - one who is the consort of Lord *Śiva*; *jñānavairāgyasiddhyartham* - for the purpose of gaining dispassion and knowledge; *bhikṣām* - *bhikṣā*; *dehi* - give; *ca* - and; *pārvatī* - O *Pārvatī*!

O *Annapūrṇā*! who is always full! O *Pārvatī*! who is the consort of Lord *Śiva*. May you give *bhikṣā*, food, for the purpose of gaining dispassion and knowledge.

माता च पार्वतीदेवी पिता देवो महेश्वरः ।
बान्धवाः शिवभक्ताश्च स्वदेशो भुवनत्रयम् ॥ १२॥

mātā ca pārvatīdevī pitā devo maheśvaraḥ
bāndhavāḥ śivabhaktāśca svadeśo bhuvanatryam (12)

mātā - mother; *ca pārvatī* - *Pārvatī*; *devī* - Goddess; *pitā* - father; *devāḥ* - Lord; *maheśvaraḥ* - *Śiva*; *bāndhavāḥ* - relatives; *śivabhaktāḥ* - are devotees of Lord *Śiva*; *ca* - and; *svadeśaḥ* - abode is; *bhuvanatryam* - the three worlds.

My mother is Goddess *Pārvatī*. Father is Lord *Śiva*. My relatives are devotees of Lord *Śiva* and my abode is the three worlds.

Śrī Nāma Rāmāyaṇa बाल काण्डः *Bāla Kāṇḍaḥ*

१. शुद्धब्रह्म परात्पर राम *śuddhabrahmaparātpara* *rāma*
O *Rāma*, one who is pure *brahman* and is greater than the unmanifest (*māyā*)!

२. कालात्मकपरमेश्वरú राम *kālātmakaparameśvara* *rāma*
O *Rāma*, one who is the Lord *Śiva* and one whose nature is time!

३. शेषतल्पसुखनिद्रित राम *śeṣatalpasukhanidrita* *rāma*
O *Rāma*, one who was reclined on the bed of the king of serpents!

४. ब्रह्माद्यमरप्रार्थित राम *brahmādyamaraprārthita* *rāma*
O *Rāma*, one who was prayed to by the deities beginning from Lord *Brahmā*!

५. चण्डकिरणकुलमण्डन राम *caṇḍakiraṇakulamaṇḍana* *rāma*
O *Rāma*, one who made the solar dynasty very famous!

६. श्रीमद्दशरथनन्दन राम *śrīmaddaśarathanandana* *rāma*
O *Rāma*, who was the son of *Śrī Daśaratha*!

७. कौसल्यासुखवर्धन राम *kausalyāsukhavardhana* *rāma*
O *Rāma*, who enhanced the joy of *Kausalyā*!

८. विश्वामित्रप्रियधन राम *viśvāmitrapriyadhana* *rāma*
O *Rāma*, who was dear to Sage *Viśvāmitra*!

९. घोरताटकाघातक राम *ghoratāṭakāghātaka* *rāma*
O *Rāma*, who was the killer of the terrible *Tāṭakā*!

१०. मारीचादिनिपातकò राम *mārīcādinipātaka* *Rāma*
O *Rāma*, who was the destroyer of demons like *Mārīca*!

११. कौशिकमकसंरक्षक राम *kauśikamakasamrakṣaka* *rāma*
O *Rāma*, who was the killer of the protecter of *Viśvāmitra's* sacrifice!

१२. श्रीमदहल्योद्धारक राम *śrīmadahalyoddhāraka* *rāma*
O *Rāma*, who was the uplifter of *Ahalyā*!

१३. गौतममुनिसंपूजित राम *gautamamunisampūjita* *rāma*
O *Rāma*, who was worshipped by sages like *Gautama*!

१४. सुरमुनिवरगणसंस्तुत राम *suramunivaragaṇasaṃstuta* *rāma*
O *Rāma*, who was praised by a host of great sages of heaven!

१५. नाविकधावितमृदुपद राम *nāvikadhāvitamṛdupada* *rāma*
O *Rāma*, who has feet that jumped over the waters while navigating!

१६. मिथिलापुरजनमोहक *mithilāpurajanamohaka* *rāma*
O *Rāma*, who attracted the people of the city of *Mithilā*!

१७. विदेहमानसरञ्जक राम *videhamānasarañjaka* *rāma*
O *Rāma*, who delighted the mind of King *Janaka*!

१८. त्रयम्बककार्मुकभञ्जक राम *tryambakakārmukabhañjaka* *rāma*
O *Rāma*, who broke the bow of Lord *Śiva*!

१९. सीतार्पितवरमालिक राम *sītārpitavaramālika* *rāma*
O *Rāma*, who wore the garland offered by *Sītā*!

२०. कृतवैवाहिककौतुक राम *kṛtavaivāhikakautuka* *rāma*
O *Rāma*, who was full of joy born of his marriage (to *Sītā*)!

२१. भार्गवदर्पविनाशक राम *bhārgavadarpavināśaka* *rāma*
O *Rāma*, who eliminated the pride of *Paraśurāma*!

२२. श्रीमदयोध्यापालक राम *śrīmadayodhyāpālaka* *Rāma*
O *Rāma*, who was the protector of *Ayodhyā*!

अयोध्या काण्डः *Ayodhyā Kāṇḍaḥ*

२३. अगणितगुणगणभूषित राम *aganitagunaganabhūṣita* *rāma*

O *Rāma*, who was endowed with countless virtues!

२४. अवनीतनयाकामित राम *avanītanayākāmita* *rāma*

O *Rāma*, who was loved by *Sītā*, daughter of Earth!

२५. राकाचन्द्रसमानन राम *rākācandrasamānana* *rāma*

O *Rāma*, who has a face like the moon on a full moon day!

२६. पितृवाक्याश्रितकानन राम *pitṛvākyāśritakānana* *rāma*

O *Rāma*, who went to the forest resorting to his father's words!

२७. प्रियगुहविनिवेदितपद राम *priyaguhaviniveditapada* *rāma*

O *Rāma*, whose feet were worshipped by *Guha*!

२८. तत्क्षालितनिजमृदुपद राम *tatkṣālitanijamṛdupada* *rāma*

O *Rāma*, whose soft feet were washed by *Guha*!

२९. भरद्वाजमुखानन्दक राम *bharadvājamukhānandaka* *rāma*

O *Rāma*, who gave joy to *Bharadvāja*!

३०. चित्रकूटाद्रिनिकेतन राम *citrakūṭādriniketana* *rāma*

O *Rāma*, who dwelt in the mountain of *Citrakūṭa*!

३१. दशरथसंततचिन्तित राम *daśrathasantatacintita* *rāma*

O *Rāma*, who was constantly remembered by *Daśaratha*!

३२. कैकेयीतनयार्थित राम *kaikeyītanayārthita* *rāma*

O *Rāma*, one who was sought after by *Bharata*, the son of *Kaikeyī*!

३३. विरचितनिजपितृकर्मक राम *virascitanijapitṛkarmaka* *rāma*

O *Rāma*, by whom the rites for his father was done!

३४. भरतार्पितनिजपादुक राम *bharatārpitanijapāduka* *rāma*

O *Rāma*, by whom (his own) sandals were given to *Bharata*!

अरण्य काण्डः — *Aranya Kāndaḥ*

३५. दण्डकावनजनपावन राम *daṇḍakāvanajanapāvana rāma*
O *Rāma*, who blessed the people of *Daṇḍaka* forest!

३६. दुष्टविराधविनाशन राम *duṣṭavirādhavināśana rāma*
O *Rāma*, who destroyed the wicked *Virādha*!

३७. शरभङ्गसुतीक्ष्ण अर्चित राम *śarabhaṅgasutīkṣṇa arcita rāma*
O *Rāma*, who was worshipped by *Śarabhaṅga* and *Sutīkṣṇa*!

३८. अगस्त्यानुग्रहवर्धित राम *agastyānugrahavardhita rāma*
O *Rāma*, who grew in stature by the blessing of Sage *Agastya*!

३९. गृध्राधिपसंसेवित राम *gṛdhrādhipasaṃsevita rāma*
O *Rāma*, who was served by the king of vultures *Jaṭāyu*!

४०. पञ्चवटीतटसुस्थित राम *pañcavaṭītaṭasusthita rāma*
O *Rāma*, who dwelt happily on the bank of *Pañcavaṭī*!

४१. शूर्पणखार्तिविधायक राम *śūrpaṇakhārtividhāyaka rāma*
O *Rāma*, who caused suffering to *Śūrpaṇakhā*!

४२. खरदूषणमुखसूदक राम *kharadūṣaṇamukhasūdaka rāma*
O *Rāma*, who destroyed the demons like *Khara* and *Dūṣaṇa*!

४३. सीताप्रियहरिणानुग राम *sītāpriyahariṇānuga rāma*
O *Rāma*, who went after the deer which was dear to *Sītā*!

४४. मारीचार्तिकृदाशुग राम *mārīcārtikṛtāśuga rāma*
O *Rāma*, whose arrow is the tormenter *Mārīca*!

४५. विनष्टसीतान्वेषकô राम *vinaṣṭasītānveṣaka rāma*
O *Rāma*, who searched for the lost *Sītā*!

४६. गृध्राधिपगतिदायक राम *gṛdhrādhipagatidāyaka rāma*
O *Rāma*, who gave a good world to king of vultures, *Jaṭāyu* (on his death)!

४७. शबरीदत्तफलाशन राम *śabarīdattaphalāśana rāma*
O *Rāma*, who ate the fruits given by *Śabarī*!

४८. कबन्धबाहुच्छेदन राम *kabandhabāhucchedana rāma*

O *Rāma*, who cut the hands of *Kabandha*!

किष्किन्धा काण्डः *Kiṣkindā Kāṇḍaḥ*

४९. हनुमत्सेवितनिजपद राम *hanumatsevitanijapada* *rāma*
O *Rāma*, whose feet were served by *Hanumān*!

५०. नतसुग्रीवाभीष्टद राम *natasugrīvābhīṣṭada* *rāma*
O *Rāma*, who gave the desired things to *Sugrīva*!

५१. गर्वितवालिसंहारक राम *garvitavālisaṃhāraka* *rāma*
O *Rāma*, who destroyed the proud *Vāli*!

५२. वानरदूतप्रेषक राम *vānaradūtapreṣaka* *rāma*
O *Rāma*, who sent the monkey messenger (to find *Sītā*)!

५३. हितकरलक्ष्मणसंयुत राम *hitakaralakṣmaṇasaṃyuta* *rāma*
O *Rāma*, who was always with the helpful *Lakṣmaṇa*!

सुन्दर काण्डः *Sundara Kāṇḍaḥ*

५४. कपिवरसंततसंस्मृत राम *kapivarasantatasaṃsmṛta* *rāma*
O *Rāma*, who was remembered by *Hanumān* always!

५५. तद्गतिविघ्नध्वंसक राम *tadgativighnadhvaṃsaka* *rāma*
O *Rāma*, who destroyed all obstacles on the path of *Hanumān*!

५६. सीताप्राणधारक राम *sītāprāṇadhāraka* *rāma*
O *Rāma*, who was the supporter of *Sītā*'s life!

५७. दुष्टदशाननदूषित राम *duṣṭadaśānanadūṣita* *rāma*
O *Rāma*, who was the destroyer of the wicked *Rāvaṇa*!

५८. शिष्टहनूमद्भूषित राम *śiṣṭahanumadbhūṣita* *rāma*
O *Rāma*, who was adorned by the noble *Hanumān*!

५९. सीतावेदितकाकावन राम *sītāveditakākāvana* *rāma*
O *Rāma*, who protected *Sītā* from *Kākāsura* an incident known only to her!

६०. कृतचूडामणिदर्शन राम *kṛtacūḍāmaṇidarśana* *rāma*

O *Rāma*, who was shown the crest jewel!

६१. कपिवरवचनाश्वासित राम *kapivaravacanāśvāsita* *rāma*

O *Rāma*, who was consoled by the words of *Hanumān*!

युद्ध काण्डः *Yuddha Kāṇḍaḥ*

६२. रावणनिधनप्रस्थित राम *rāvaṇanindhanaprasthita* *rāma*

O *Rāma*, who started (for the battlefield) in order kill *Rāvaṇa*!

६३. वानरसैन्यसमावृत राम *vānarasainyasamāvṛta* *rāma*

O *Rāma*, who was surrounded by the army of monkeys!

६४. शोषितसरिदीशार्थित राम *śoṣitasaridīśārthita* *rāma*

O *Rāma*, who was prayed to by the deity of ocean, who had dried up!

६५. विभीषणाभयदायक राम *vibhīṣaṇābhayadāyaka* *rāma*

O *Rāma*, who gave fearlessness to *Vibhīṣaṇa*!

६६. पर्वतसेतुनिबन्धक राम *parvatasetunibhandhaka* *rāma*

O *Rāma*, who bound the ocean with a stone-bridge!

६७. कुम्भकर्णशिरश्छेदक राम *kumbhakarṇaśiraśchedaka* *rāma*

O *Rāma*, who cut asunder the head of *Kumbhakarṇa*!

६८. राक्षससङ्घविमर्दक राम *rākṣasasaṅgavimardaka* *rāma*

O *Rāma*, who annihilated the host of demons!

६९. अहिमहिरावणचारण राम *ahimahirāvaṇacāraṇa* *rāma*

O *Rāma*, who had *Ahimahirāvaṇa* as a messenger!

७०. संहृतदशमुखरावण राम *saṃhṛtadaśamukharāvaṇa* *rāma*

O *Rāma*, who destroyed the ten-headed *Rāvaṇa*!

७१. विधिभवमुखसुरसंस्तुत राम *vidhibhavamukhasurasaṃstuta* *rāma*

O *Rāma*, who was praised by *Brahmā*, *Śiva* and so on!

७२. खस्थितदशरथवीक्षित राम *khasthitadaśarathavīkṣita* *rāma*

O *Rāma*, who was seen by *Daśaratha* from the heavens!

७३. सीतादर्शनमोदित राम *sītādarśanamodita* *rāma*

O *Rāma*, who was delighted at the sight of *Sītā* !

७४. अभिषिक्तविभीषणनत राम *abhiṣiktavibhīṣaṇanata* *rāma*

O *Rāma*, who was saluted by the coronated king *Vibhīṣaṇa*!

७५. पुष्पकयानारोहण राम *puṣpakayānārohaṇa* *rāma*

O *Rāma*, who ascended the *puṣpaka* chariot!

७६. भरद्वाजाभिनिषेवण राम *bharadvājābhiniṣevaṇa* *rāma*

O *Rāma*, who served *Bharadvāja* well!

७७. भरतप्राणप्रियकरú राम *bharataprāṇapriyakara* *rāma*

O *Rāma*, who was dear to *Bharata's* life!

७८. साकेतपुरीभूषण राम *sāketapurībhūṣaṇa* *rāma*

O *Rāma*, who was the ornament of *Ayodhyā*!

७९. सकलस्वीयसमानन राम *sakalasvīyasamānana* *rāma*

O *Rāma*, who looked upon all as equal to himself!

८०. रत्नलसत्पीठास्थित राम *ratnalasatpīṭhāsthita* *rāma*

O *Rāma*, who was seated on a diamond throne!

८१. पट्टाभिषेकालङ्कृत राम *paṭṭābhiṣekālaṅkṛta* *rāma*

O *Rāma*, who was adorned with the crown!

८२. पार्थिवकुलसंमानित राम *pārthivakulasammānita* *rāma*

O *Rāma*, who was honoured by all the kings!

८३. विभीषणार्पितरङ्गक राम *vibhīṣaṇārpitaraṅgaka* *rāma*

O *Rāma*, who offered Lord *Raṅganātha* to *Vibhīṣaṇa* for worship!

८४. कीशकुलानुग्रहकरú राम *kīśakulānugrahakara* *rāma*

O *Rāma*, who blessed the lineage of monkeys!

८५. सकलजीवसंरक्षक राम *sakalajīvasaṃrakṣaka* *rāma*

O *Rāma*, who is the protector of all *jīvas*!

८६. समस्तलोकाधारक राम *samastalokhādhāraka* *rāma*
O *Rāma*, who is the support of all the worlds!

८७. आगतमुनिगणसंस्तुत राम *āgatamunigaṇasaṃstuta* *rāma*
O *Rāma*, who was praised by the sages who came (to witness the war)!

उत्तर काण्डः *Uttara Kāṇḍaḥ*

८८. विश्रुतदशकण्ठोद्भव राम *viśrutadaśakaṇṭhodbhava* *rāma*
O *Rāma*, who was proclaimed by famous *Rāvaṇa*!

८९. सीतालिङ्गननिर्वृत राम *sītāliṅgananirvṛta* *rāma*
O *Rāma*, who was fulfilled in the embrace of *Sītā*!

९०. नीतिसुरक्षितजनपद राम *nītisurakṣitajanapada* *rāma*
O *Rāma*, who ruled his kingdom righteously!

९१. विपिनत्याजितजनकज राम *vipinatyājitajanakaja* *rāma*
O *Rāma*, who left *Sītā* in the forest!

९२. कारितलवणासुरवध राम *kāritalavaṇāsuravadha* *rāma*
O *Rāma*, who did the killing of *Lavaṇāsura*!

९३. स्वर्गतशम्बुकसंस्तुत राम *svargataśambuka saṃstuta* *rāma*
O *Rāma*, who was praised by *Śambuka* who gained heaven!

९४. स्वतनयकुशलवनन्दित राम *svatanayakuślavanandita* *rāma*
O *Rāma*, who was delighted by his sons *Kuśa* and *Lava*!

९५. अश्वमेधक्रतुदीक्षित राम *aśvamedhakratudīkṣita* *rāma*
O *Rāma*, who took the vow of *Aśvamedha* sacrifice!

९६. कालावेदितसुरपद राम *kālaveditasurapada* *rāma*
O *Rāma*, who reached heavens as ordained by time!

९७. आयोध्यकजनमुक्तिद राम *āyodhyakajanamuktida* *rāma*
O *Rāma*, who gave *mokṣa* to the people of *Ayodhyā*!

९८. विधिमुखविबुधानन्दक राम *vidhimukhavibhudhānandaka rāma*
O *Rāma*, who gave happiness to *Brahmā* and other men of wisdom!

९९. तेजोमयनिजरूपक राम *tejomayanijarūpaka rāma*
O *Rāma*, whose nature is awareness!

१००. संसृतिबन्धविमोचक राम *saṃsṛtibandhavimocaka rāma*
O *Rāma*, who releases one from the bondage of *saṃsāra*!

१०१. धर्मस्थापनतत्पर राम *dharmasthāpanatatpara rāma*
O *Rāma*, who is committed to establishment of *dharma*!

१०२. भक्तिपरायणमुक्तिद राम *bhaktiparāyaṇamuktida rāma*
O *Rāma*, who gives *mokṣa* to those whose goal is devotion!

१०३. सर्वचराचरपालक राम *sarvacarācarapālaka rāma*
O *Rāma*, who protects the moving and non-moving beings!

१०४. सर्वभवामयवारक राम *sarvabhyāmayavāraka rāma*
O *Rāma*, who removes the disease of repeated birth!

१०५. वैकुण्ठालयसंस्थित राम *vaikuṇṭhālayasaṃsthita rāma*
O *Rāma*, who is seated in the abode of *vaikuṇṭha*!

१०६. नित्यानन्दपदस्थित राम *nithyānandapadasthita rāma*
O *Rāma*, who is established in eternal happiness!

१०७. राम राम जय राजा राम *rāma rāma jaya rājā rāma*
Victory unto you King *Rāma*!

१०८. राम राम जय सीता राम *rāma rāma jaya sītā rāma*
Victory unto you, *Sītārāma*!

राम राम जय राजा राम *rāma rāma jaya rājā rāma*
Victory unto you King *Rāma*!

राम राम जय सीता राम *rāma rāma jaya sītā rāma*
Victory unto you, *Sītārāma*!

राम राम जय राजा राम *rāma rāma jaya rājā rāma*

Victory unto you King *Rāma*!

राम राम जय सीता राम *rāma rāma jaya sītā rāma*

Victory unto you, *Sītārāma*!

Śrī Hanumān Cālīsā

श्रीगुरु चरन सरोज रज	*śrīguru caran saroj raj*
निज मन मुकुरु सुधारि ।	*nij man mukuru sudhāri*
बरनउँ रघुबर बिमल जसु	*bharanau raghubar bimal jasu*
जो दायकु फल चारि ॥	*jo dāyak phal cāri*

After purifying the mirror of my mind with the dust of the lotus feet of *Śrī Guru*, I begin the description of the taintless glories of Lord *Rāma* that bestow the four human ends in life.

बुद्धिहीन तनु जानिके	*buddhihīn tanu jānike*
सुमिरौं पवनकुमार ।	*sumirau pavanakumār*
बल बुधि बिद्या देहु मोहिं	*balabudhi bidyā dehu mohiṃ*
हरहु कलेस बिकार ॥	*harahu kales bikār*

O Lord *Hanumān*! The son of wind deity! You know me with the shortcomings of my intellect. Please remove all afflictions and defects in me, and grant me the strength of body, intelligence and knowledge.

चौपाई	*caupāī*
जय हनुमान ज्ञानगुन सागर ।	*jay hanumān jñānaguna sāgar*
जय कपीस तिहुँ लोक उजागर ॥१॥	*jay kapīsa tihu lok ujāgar* (1)

Victory unto you O *Hanumān*! The ocean of wisdom and virtue! O Lord of the monkeys! The illuminator of the three worlds!

राम दूत अतुलित बल धामा ।	*rāma dūta atulita bala dhāmā*
अंजनिपुत्र पवनसुत नामा ॥२॥	*añjaniputra pavanasuta nāmā* (2)

O messenger of Lord *Rāma*! O abode of incomparable strength! O son of *Añjanā*! O *Pavanasuta*, son of wind deity!

महाबीर बिक्रम बजरंगी ।	*mahābīra bikrama bajaraṅgī*
कुमति निवार सुमति के संगी ॥३॥	*kumati nivāra sumati ke saṅgī* (3)

You are a great warrior with a body having the power of a thunderbolt. You are the remover of negative tendencies and the companion of noble thoughts.

कंचन बरन बिराज सुबेसा ।	*kañcana barana birāja subesā*
कानन कुंडल कुंचित केसा ॥४॥	*kānana kuṇḍala kuñcita kesā* (4)

You have the golden hue and you shine in beautiful clothes. You wear ornamental earrings. You have fine curly hair.

हाथ बज्र औ ध्वजा बिराजै ।	*hāth bajra au dhvajā birājai*
काँधे मूज जनेऊ साजै ॥ ५॥	*kām̐dhe mūm̐ja janeu sājai* (5)

You shine with flag and thunderbolt in your hands, and with the sacred thread made of *mūnja* grass across your shoulders.

संकर सुवन केसरीनंदन ।	*saṅkara suvan kesarīnandan*
तेज प्रताप महा जग बंदन ॥६॥	*tej pratāp mahā jag bandan* (6)

O incarnation of Lord *Śiva* and son of *Kesari*! You are adored by the entire universe for your radiance and valour.

बिद्यावान गुनी अति चातुर ।	*bidyāvān gunī ati cātur*
राम काज करिबे को आतुर ॥७ ॥	*rām kāj karibe ko ātur* (7)

You are learned, virtuous, extremely skilled and waiting to carry out the work of *Śrī Rāma.*

प्रभु चरित्र सुनिबे को रसिया ।	*prabu caritra sunibe ko rasiyā*
राम लखन सीता मन बसिया ॥ ८॥	*rām lakhan sītā mana basiyā* (8)

You enjoy listening to the glories of your master. You have *Rāma, Lakṣmaṇa* and *Sītā* abiding in your mind.

सूक्ष्म रूप धरि सियहिं दिखावा ।	*sūkṣm rūp dhari siyahiṃ dikhāvā*
बिकट रूपधरि लंक जरावा ॥९॥	*bikat rūp dhari laṅka jarāvā* (9)

Assuming a tiny form you showed yourself to *Sītā*. Assuming a contrary form, you burnt the city of *Laṅkā.*

भीम रूपधरि असुर सँहारे।	*bhim rūp dhari asur sam̐hāre*
रामचंद्र के काज सँवारे ॥१०॥	*rāmacandra ke kāj samvāre* (10)

Assuming a gigantic form, you destroyed the demons and fulfilled the tasks of *Śrī Rāma.*

लाय सजीवन लखन जियाये ।
श्रीरघुबीर हरषि उर लाये।। ११।।

lāy sajīvan lakhan jiyāye
śrīraghubīr harasi ur lāye (11)

When you brought the *sañjīva* herb (along with the hill) for saving *Lakṣmaṇa, Śrī Rāma* embraced you with joy.

रघुपति कीन्ही बहुत बडाई।
तुम मम प्रिय भरत हि सम भाई।। १२।।

raghupati kīnhī bahut baḍāī
tum mam priya bharata hi sama bhāī (12)

Śrī Rāma praised you profusely and said that you are a dear brother to him like *Bharata.*

सहस बदन तुम्हरो जस गावैं ।
अस कहि श्रीपति कंठ लगावैं ।। १३।।

sahasa badan tumharo jasa gāvaiṃ
as kahi śrīpati kaṇath lagāvaṃ (13)

Śrī Rāma embracing you over your shoulder, said that even the thousand-hooded serpent, *Śeṣanāga*, sings your praise.

सनकादिक ब्रह्मादि मुनीसा ।
नारद सारद सहित अहीसा ।। १४।।

sanakādik brahmādi munīsā
nārada sārada sahit ahīsā (14)

जम कुबेर दिगपाल जहाँ ते ।
कबि कोबिद कहि सके कहाँ ते ।। १५।।

jam kuber digpal jahām̐ te
kabi kobid kahi sake kahām̐ (15)

The sages such as *Sanaka* etc., the Gods such as *Brahmā* etc., Sage *Nārada*, Goddess *Sarasvatī* and *Śeṣanāga*, Deity *Yama*, Deity *Kubera*, the guardian deities, poets and scholars have not been able to describe your glories fully.

तुम उपकार सुग्रीवहिं कीन्हा ।
राम मिलाए राजपद दीन्हा ।। १६।।

tum upakār sigrīvahiṃ kīnhā
rām milay rājpad dīnhā (16)

You did a great help to *Sugrīva* by introducing him to *Śrī Rāma* and restoring the throne to him.

तुम्हरो मन्त्र बिभीषन माना।
लंकेस्वर भए सब जग जाना ।।१७ ।।

tumharo mantra bibhīṣana mānā
laṅkesvar bhae sab jag jānā (17)

The whole world knows that *Vibhīṣana* accepted your advice and became the king of *Laṅkā*.

जुग सहस्र योजन पर भानू ।
लील्यो ताहि मधुर फल जानू ।।

jug sahasra yojan par bhānū
līlyo tāhi madhur phal jānū (18)

The sun is located at such a distance that it would take thousands of *yugas* to reach.. Seeing it as a sweet fruit, you took it effortlessly.

प्रभु मुद्रिका मेलिमुख माहीं ।
जलधि लाँधि गये अचरज नाहीं।। १९।।

prabhu mudrikā melimukh māhīṃ
jaladhi lām̐dhi gaye acaraj nāhīṃ (19)

That you crossed the ocean, carrying the ring of *Śrī Rāma* in your mouth is not a matter for wonder (as you are seen to be capable of such deeds in the past).

दुर्गम काज जगत के जेते ।
सुगम अनुग्रह तुम्हरे तेते ।। २०।।

durgam kāj jagata ke jete
sugam anugrah tumhare tete (20)

Whatever difficult tasks are there in the world, they become easy to perform by your grace.

राम दुआरे तुम रखवारे ।
होत न आज्ञा बिनु पैसारे ।। २१।।

rām duare tum rakhvāre
hota na ājñā bin paisāre (21)

You are the gatekeeper of *Śrī Rāma* where nobody can enter without your permission.

सब सुख लहै तुम्हारी सरना।
तुम रक्षक काहू को डरना ।।२२।।

sab sukh lahai tumhārī saranā
tum rakṣak kāhū ko ḍarnā (22)

In your refuge, one enjoys all happiness. When you are the protector, why should one be afraid.

आपन तेज सम्हारो आपै।
तीनों लोक हाँक ते काँपै ।।२३।।

āpai tej samhāro āpai
tīnoṃ lok hām̐ka te kām̐pai (23)

You alone can keep under check your force. All the three worlds tremble before your power.

भूत पिसाच निकट नहिं आवै।
महाबीर जब नाम सुनावै ।। २४।।

bhūt pisac nikaṭ nahi āvai
mahābīr jab nām sunāvai (24)

No destructive evil spirits dare to come near one who chants your name, you being a great warrior.

नासै रोग हरै सब पीरा ।
जपत निरंतर हनुमत बीरा ।।२५।।

nāsai rog harai sab pīrā
japat nirantar hanumat bīrā (25)

O Lord *Hanumān*, the warrior! All diseases get destroyed and pains disappear when your name is chanted constantly.

संकट तें हनुमान छुडावै ।
मन क्रम बचन ध्यान जो लावै ।।२३।।

saṅkaṭ teṃ hanumān chuḍāvai
mana krama bacan dhyān jo lāvai (26)

Lord *Hanumān* frees him from all hardships, the one who devotes his mind to him in deeds, words and thoughts.

सब पर राम तपस्वी राजा ।	*sab par rām tapasvī rājā*
तिन के काज सकल तुम साजा।। २७।।	*tin ke kāj sakala tum sājā* (27)

You accomplish the tasks of King *Rāma* who accomplishes the desires of ascetics.

और मनोरथ जो कोइ लावै ।	*aur manoratha jo koi lāvai*
सोइ अमित जीवन फल पावै।। २८।।	*soi amit jīvan phal pāvai* (28)

Whoever enjoys your grace, gains limiteless results in this life, whatever be the desire he entertains.

चारों जुग परताप तुम्हारा।	*caroṃ jug paratāp tumhārā*
है परसिद्ध जगत उजियारा।। २९।।	*hai parasiddh jagat ujiyārā* (29)

Your writ prevails through all the four *yugas*, time-cycle, and your glory shines in and through the world.

साधु संत के तुम रखवारे ।	*sādhu sant ke tum rakhvāre*
असुर निकंदन राम दुलारे ।। ३०।।	*asur nikandan rām dulāre* (30)

O *Rāma's* beloved! You are the protector of the saints and sages and you are the destroyer of the demons.

अष्ट सिद्धि नौ निधि के दाता।	*aṣṭ siddhi nau nidhi ke dātā*
अस बर दीन जानकी माता ।। ३१।।	*as bar dīn jānakī mātā* (31)

Mother *Sītā* has granted you the boon that you will be the giver of eight yogic powers and nine treasures.

राम रसायन तुम्हरे पासा ।	*rām rasāyan tumhare pāsā*
सदा रहो रघुपति के दासा ।। ३२।।	*sadā raho raghupati ke dāsā* (32)

You have a medicine with you which is the name of *Rāma* since you always remain surrendered to Lord *Rāma*.

तुम्हरे भजन राम को पावै।	*tumhare bhajan rām ko pāvai*
जनम जनम के दुख बिसरावै।। ३३।।	*janam janam ke dukh bisarāvai* (33)

Your worship takes one to Lord *Rāma* and sweeps away the sufferings of all the past lives.

अंत काल रघुबर पुर जाई ।	*aṃt kāl raghubar pura jāī*
जहाँ जन्म हरिभक्त कहाई ।। ३४।।	*jahām̐ janma haribhakta kahāī* (34)

At the end of his life, such a person goes to the abode of Lord *Rāma* and (if he again takes) birth, he will (continue to be called) a *haribhakta*, a devotee of Lord *Viṣṇu.*

और देवता चित्त न धरई ।	*aur devatā citta na dharaī*
हनुमत सेइ सर्ब सुख करई।। ३५।।	*hanumat sei sarb sukh karaī* (35)

To him who does not think of any deity other than *Hanumān* in his mind, all the deities bestow happiness to him.

संकट कटै मिटै सब पीरा ।	*saṅkaṭ kaṭai miṭai sab pīrā*
जो सुमिरै हनुमत बलबीरा।। ३६।।	*jo sumirai hanumat balabīrā* (36)

All difficulties are warded off and pains are removed for those who think of the all powerful *Hanumān.*

जै जै जै हनुमान गोसाईं ।	*jai jai jai hanumān gosāī*
कृपा करहु गुरु देव की नाईं ।।३७।।	*kṛpā karahu guru dev kī nāīṃ* (37)

Victory unto to you! Victory unto to you! Victory unto to you! O *Hanumān*! O Gurudev! Bless us.

जो शत बार पाट कर कोई।	*jo śat bār pāṭh kara koī*
छूटहि बंदि महा सुख होई ।।३८।।	*chūṭahi bandi mahā sukh hoi* (38)

Whoever chants this *Cālīsā* one hundred times will become freed from bondage and gain the highest happiness.

जो यह पढै हनुमान चलीसा।	*jo yaḥ paḍhai hanumān calīsā*
होय सिद्धि साखी गौरीसा ।।३९।।	*hoy siddhi sākhī gaurīsā* (39)

Whoever chants this *Hanumān Cālīsā* will gain his desired ends. Lord *Śiva* is the witness (for this statement).

तुलसीदास सदा हरि चेरा ।	*tulsīdās sadā hari cerā*
कीजै नाथ हृदय महँ डेरा ।।४०।।	*kījai nāth hṛday mahaṁ ḍerā* (40)

Tulasidas, who is ever the servant of the Lord, prays that the Lord reside in his heart.

दोहा	*dohā*
पवनतनय संकट हरन	*pavantanaya saṅkaṭ haran*
मंगल मूरति रूप।	*maṅgal mūrati rūp*
राम लषन सीता सहित ।	*rām laṣan sītā sahita*
हृदय बसहु सुर भूप।।	*hṛdaya basahu sur bhūpa*

May *Hanumān*, who removes hardships, who is an embodiment of auspiciousness, who is the Lord who protects the world, reside in my heart along with *Śrī Rāma*, *Lakṣmaṇa* and *Sītā*.

सियावर रामचन्द्र की जय	*siyāvara rāmacandra kī jaya*
पवनसुत हनूमान की जय	*pavanasuta hanūmān ki jaya*
उमापति महादेव की जय	*umāpati mahādeva kī jaya*
बोलो भाई सब सन्तन की जय	*bolo bhāī sab santān kī jaya*

O Brother, proclaim 'Victory to Lord *Rāma*, bridegroom of *Sītā*'. 'Victory to Lord *Hanumān*, son of wind deity'. 'Victory to Lord *Śiva*, Lord of *Pārvatī*. 'Victory to all saints'!

Gītā Dhyānam

ॐ पार्थाय प्रतिबोधितां भगवता नारायणेन स्वयं
व्यासेन ग्रथितां पुराणमुनिना मध्येमहाभारतम् ।
अद्वैतामृतवर्षिणीं भगवतीमष्टादशाध्यायिनीम्
अम्ब त्वामनुसन्दधामि भगवद्गीते भवद्वेषिणीम् ॥१॥

oṃ pārthāya pratibodhitāṃ bhagavatā nārāyaṇenasvayaṃ
vyāsena grathitāṃ purāṇamuninā madhyemahābhāratam
advaitāmṛtavarṣiṇīṃ bhagavatīmaṣṭādaśādhyāyinīm
amba tvāmanusandadhāmi bhagavadgīte bhavadveṣiṇīm (1)

om - *om*; *pārthāya* - for the sake of *Arjuna*, the son of *Pṛthā* (*Kuntī*); *pratibodhitām* - taught; *bhagavatā* - by Lord; *nārāyaṇena* - by *Nārāyaṇa*; *svayaṃ* - himself; *vyāsena* - by *Vyāsa*; *grathitām*- faithfully collected and reported; *purāṇa-muninā* - by the ancient sage; *madhye-mahābhāratam* - in the middle of the *Mahābhārata*; *advaita-amṛtavarṣiṇīm* - showering the nectar of nonduality; *bhagavatīm* - the Goddess; *aṣṭādaśa-adhyāyinīm* - of eighteen chapters; *amba* - O Mother; *tvām* - you; *anusandadhāmi* - I repeatedly invoke; *bhagavadgīte* - O *Bhagavad-gītā*; *bhava-dveṣiṇīm* - destroyer of the life of becoming

Om. O Goddess Mother, O *Bhagavad Gītā*; taught by Lord *Nārāyaṇa* himself for the sake of *Arjuna*, the son of *Pṛthā* (*Kuntī*), faithfully collected and reported by the ancient Sage *Vyāsa*, (and placed) in the middle of *Mahābhārata*, comprised of eighteen chapters, showering the nectar of nonduality, the destroyer of the life of becoming, I invoke you again and again.

नमोऽस्तु ते व्यास विशालबुद्धे फुल्लारविन्दायतपत्रनेत्र ।
येन त्वया भारततैलपूर्णः प्रज्वालितोज्ञानमयः प्रदीपः ॥२॥

namo'stu te vyāsa viśālabuddhe phullāravindāyatapatranetra
yena tvayā bhāratatailapūrṇaḥ prajvālitojñānamayaḥ pradīpaḥ (2)

namaḥ - salutation; *astu* - let it be; *te* - to you; *vyāsa* - O *Vyāsa*; *viśālabuddhe* - one whose intellect is vast; *phulla-aravinda-āyata-patra-netra* - one whose eyes are clear and pleasing like a fully bloomed lotus; *yena* - by whom; *tvayā* - by you; *bhārata-taila-pūrṇaḥ* - that which is filled with the oil of the *Bhārata*; *prajvālitaḥ* - well lighted; *jñānamayaḥ* - in the form of knowledge; *pradīpaḥ* - the lamp

O *Vyāsa*, the one whose intellect is vast, whose eyes are clear and as pleasing as a fully bloomed lotus, who lit the lamp of knowledge well, by filling it with the oil of the *Mahābhārata*, unto you, (my) salutations.

प्रपन्नपारिजाताय तोत्रवेत्रैकपाणये ।
ज्ञानमुद्राय कृष्णाय गीतामृतदुहे नमः ॥ ३ ॥

prapannapārijātāya totravetraikapāṇaye
jnānamudrāya kṛṣṇāya gītāmṛtaduhe namaḥ (3)

prapannapārijātāya - unto the one who is the wish-fulfilling tree for those who have surrendered; *totra-vetraika-pāṇaye* - unto the one who has the whip in one hand; *jnānamudrāya* - the one whose other hand assumes the gesture symbolising knowledge; *kṛṣṇāya* - unto that *Kṛṣṇa*; *gītā-amṛta-duhe* - the one who milks the nectar of *Gītā*; *namaḥ* - (my) salutation

Unto Lord *Kṛṣṇa* who is the wish-fulfilling tree for those who have surrendered, who has the whip in one hand, and the symbol of knowledge in the other, (and) who milks the nectar that is *Gītā*, (my) salutations.

सर्वोपनिषदो गावः दोग्धा गोपालनन्दनः।
पार्थो वत्सः सुधीर्भोक्ता दुग्धं गीतामृतं महत् ॥ ४ ॥

sarvopaniṣado gāvaḥ dogdhā gopālanandanaḥ
pārtho vatsaḥ sudhīrbhoktā dugdhaṃ gītāmṛtaṃ mahat (4)

sarva-upaniṣadaḥ - all the *Upaniṣads*; *gāvaḥ* - cows; *dogdhā* - one who milks; *gopāla-nandanaḥ* - son of the nourisher and protector of cows; *pārthaḥ* - *Arjuna*; *vatsaḥ* - calf; *sudhīḥ* - one whose mind is clear; *bhoktā* - enjoyer; *dugdham* - milk; *gītā-amṛtam* - nectar of the *Gītā*; *mahat* - great (invaluable)

The *Upaniṣads* are the cow, the son of cowherd (*Kṛṣṇa*) is the miler, *Arjuna* is the calf, the one whose mind is clear is the drinker, and the invaluable, timeless *Gītā* is the milk.

वसुदेवसुतं देवं कंसचाणूरमर्दनम्।
देवकी परमानन्दं कृष्णं वन्दे जगद्गुरुम्।। ५ ।।

vasudevasutaṃ devaṃ kaṃsacāṇūramardanam

devakī paramānandaṃ kṛṣṇaṃ vande jagadgurum (5)

vasudevasutam - son of *Vasudeva*; *devam* - the Lord; *kaṃsa-cāṇūra-mardanam* - destroyer of *Kaṃsa* and *Cāṇūra* (demonic kings); *devakī-paramānandam* - the greatest joy of *Devakī* (*Kṛṣṇa's* mother); *kṛṣṇam* - *Kṛṣṇa*; *vande* - I salute; *jagadgurum* - teacher of the world

I salute *Kṛṣṇa*, the Lord, teacher of the world, son of *Vasudeva*, destroyer of *Kaṃsa* and *Cāṇūra*, and the greatest joy of *Devakī*.

भीष्मद्रोणतटा जयद्रथजला गान्धारनीलोत्पला
शल्यग्राहवती कृपेण वहनी कर्णेन वेलाकुला ।।
अश्वत्थामविकर्णघोरमकरा दुर्योधनावर्तिनी
सोत्तीर्णा खलु पाण्डवै रणनदी कैवर्तकः केशवः ।।६।।

bhīṣmadroṇataṭā jayadrathajalā gāndhāranīlotpalā
śalyagrāhavatī kṛpeṇa vahanī karṇena velākulā
aśvatthāmavikarṇaghoramakarā duryodhanāvrtinī
sottīrṇā khalu pāṇḍavai raṇanadī kaivartakaḥ keśavaḥ (6)

bhīṣmadroṇataṭā - with *Bhīṣma* and *Droṇa* as its banks; *jayadrathajalā* - with *Jayadratha* as its water; *gāndhāranīlotpalā* - with *Gāndhāra* as the blue lily; *śalyagrāhavatī* - with *Śalya* as the shark; *kṛpeṇa vahanī* - with *Kṛpa* as the speed of the water's flow; *karṇena velākulā* - with *Karṇa* as its breakers; *aśvatthāma vikarṇaghoramakarā* - with *Aśvatthāma* and *Vikarṇa* as its killer whales; *duryodhanāvartinī* - (and) with *Duryodhana* as its whirlpools; *sT* - that (river); *uttīrṇā* - crossed over; *khalu* - indeed; *pāṇḍavaiḥ* - by the *Pāṇḍavas*; *raṇanadī* - river of battle; *kaivartakaḥ* - the boatman; *keśavaḥ* - Lord *Kṛṣṇa*

The river of battle with *Bhīṣma* and *Droṇa* as its banks, *Jayadratha* as its water, *Gāndhāra* as the blue lily, *Śalya* as the shark, *Kṛpa* as the speed of the water's flow, *Karṇa* as its breakers, *Aśvatthāma* and *Vikarṇa* as its killer whales, and *Duryodhana* as its whirlpools, was crossed over by the *Pāṇḍavas*, whose boatman was Lord *Kṛṣṇa*.

पाराशर्यवचस्सरोजममलं गीतार्थगन्धोत्कटं
नानाख्यानककेसरं हरिकथासम्बोधनाबोधितम् ।
लोके सज्जनषट्पदैरहरहः पेपीयमानं मुदा
भूयाद्भारतपङ्कजं कलिमलप्रध्वंसि नः श्रेयसे ।।७।।

pārāśaryavacassarojamamalaṃ gītārthagandhotkaṭaṃ
nānākhyānakakesaraṃ harikathāsambodhanābodhitam
loke sajjanaṣatpadairaharahaḥ pepīyamānaṃ mudā
bhūyādbhāratapaṅkajaṃ kalimalapradhvaṃsi naḥ śreyase (7)

pārāśarya-vacas-sarojam - the lotus born of the waters of the words of the son of *Pārāśara* (*Vyāsa*); *amalaṃ* - spotless; *gītā-artha-gandha-utkaṭam* - having the *Gītā* as its sweet fragrance; *nānā-ākhyānaka-kesaram* - with many stories as its stamens; *hari-kathā-sambodhana-ābodhitam* - fully opened by the revealing stories of Lord *Hari*; *loke sajjanaṣaṭpadaiḥ raharahaḥ sajjanaṣatpadaiḥ* - by the honey bees who are right thinking people in the world; *aharahaḥ* - day after day; *pepīyamānam* - relished; *mudā* - happily; *bhūyāt* - may it be; *bhāratapaṅkajam* - the lotus of *Mahābhārata*; *kali-mala-pradhvaṃsi* - the destroyer of the blemishes of *Kali-yuga*; *naḥ* - for us; *śreyase* - for the good

May the spotless lotus, *Mahābhārata*, born of the waters of the words of the son of *Pārāśara* (*Vyāsa*), having the meaning of the *Gītā* as its sweet fragrance, with its many stories as stamens, fully opened by the revealing stories of the Lord *Hari*, relished happily day after day by the honey bees who are the right thinking people of the world, the destroyer of the blemishes of *Kali-yuga* - may it be for the good of us.

मूकं करोति वाचालं पङ्गुं लङ्घयते गिरिम्।
यत्कृपा तमहं वन्दे परमानन्दमाधवम् ॥८॥

mūkaṃ karoti vācālaṃ paṅguṃ laṅghayate girim
yatkṛpā tamahaṃ vande paramānandamādhavam (8)

mūkam - the mute; *karoti* - makes; *vācālam* - eloquent; *paṅgum* - one who is lame; *laṅghayate* - causes to scale; *girim* - mountain; *yat-kṛpā* - whose grace; *tam* - him; *aham* - I; *vande* - salute *paramānandamādhavam* - *Kṛṣṇa*, the Lord of *Lakṣmī* (wealth), whose nature is fullness

I salute *Kṛṣṇa*, the Lord of *Lakṣmī* (wealth), whose nature is fullness, whose grace makes even the mute, eloquent and the lame to scale mountaintops.

यं ब्रह्मा वरुणेन्द्ररुद्रमरुतः स्तुन्वन्ति दिव्यैस्स्तवैः
वेदैस्साङ्गपदक्रमोपनिषदैः गायन्ति यं सामगाः।
ध्यानावस्थिततद्गतेन मनसा पश्यन्ति यं योगिनः
यस्यान्तं न विदुस्सुरासुरगणाः देवाय तस्मै नमः ॥९॥

yam brahmā varuṇendrarudramarutaḥ stunvanti divyaisstavaiḥ
vedaissāṅgapadakramopaniṣadaiḥ gāyanti yaṃ sāmagāḥ
dhyānāvashtitatadgatena manasā paśyanti yaṃ yoginaḥ
yasyāntaṃ na vidussurāsuragaṇāḥ devāya tasmai namaḥ (9)

yam - whom; *brahmā* - *Brahmā*; *varuṇa-indra-rudra-marutaḥ* - *Varuṇa*, *Indra*, *Rudra* and *Marut*; *stunvanti* - sing in praise; *divyaiḥ-stavaiḥ* - with divine hymns; *vedaiḥ* - by the *Vedas*; *sa-aṅga-pada-krama-upaniṣadaiḥ* - with a full complement of the limbs (of singing) in the order of the *pada* and *krama* and the *Upaniṣads*; *gāyanti* - sing in praise; *yam* - whom; *sāmagāḥ* - the singers of the *Sāma Veda*; *dhyānāvasthita-tad-gatena manasā* - with a mind resolved in him in a state of meditation; *paśyanti* - see clearly; *yam* - whom; *yoginaḥ* - contemplative people; *yasya* - whose; *antam* - nature; *na viduḥ* - do not know; *sura-asura-gaṇāḥ* - the celestials and the demons; *devāya* - to the Lord; *tasmai* - unto him; *namaḥ* - (my) salutation

The Lord about whom *Brahmā*, *Varuṇa*, *Indra*, *Rudra* and *Marut* sing divine hymns of praise, the one whom the singers of the *Sāma Veda* praise by singing with a full complement of the limbs (of singing), in the order of the *pada* and *krama* and the *Upaniṣads*, the one who is seen clearly by contemplative people with minds resolved in him in a state of meditation, whose nature the celestials and the demons do not know, unto that Lord (my) salutations.

Bhagavad *Gītā* Ch.2

सञ्जय उवाच

तं तथा कृपयाविष्टम् अश्रुपूर्णाकुलेक्षणम् ।
विषीदन्तमिदं वाक्यम् उवाच मधुसूदनः ॥१॥

sañjaya uvāca

taṃ tathā kṛpayāviṣṭam aśrupūrṇākulekṣaṇam
viṣīdantamidaṃ vākyam uvāca madhusūdanaḥ (1)

श्री भगवान् उवाच

कुतस्त्वा कश्मलमिदं विषमे समुपस्थितम् ।
अनार्यजुष्टमस्वर्ग्यम् अकीर्तिकरमर्जुन ॥२॥

क्लैब्यं मा स्म गमः पार्थ नैतत्त्वय्युपपद्यते ।
क्षुद्रं हृदयदौर्बल्यं त्यक्त्वोत्तिष्ठ परन्तप ॥३॥

śrī bhagavān uvāca

kutastvā kaśmalamidaṃ viṣame saupasthitam
anāryajuṣṭamasvargyam akīrtikaramarjuna (2)

klaibyaṃ mā sma gamaḥ pārtha naitattvayyupapadyate
kṣudraṃ hṛdayadaurbalyaṃ tyaktvottiṣṭha parantapa (3)

अर्जुन उवाच

कथं भीष्ममहं सङ्ख्ये द्रोणं च मधुसूदन ।
इषुभिः प्रतियोत्स्यामि पूजार्हावरिसूदन ।।४।।

arjuna uvāca

kathaṃ bhīṣmamahaṃ saṅkhye droṇaṃ ca madhusūdana
iṣubhiḥ pratiyotsyāmi pūjārhāvarisūdana (4)

गुरूनहत्वा हि महानुभावान् श्रेयो भोक्तुं भैक्ष्यमपीह लोके ।
हत्वार्थकामांस्तु गुरूनिहैव
भुञ्जीय भोगान् रुधिरप्रदिग्धान् ।। ५।।

gurūnahatvā hi mahānubhāvān
śreyo bhoktuṃ bhaikṣyamapīha loke
hatvārthakāmāṃstu gurūnihaiva
bhuñjīya bhogān rudhirapradigdhān (5)

न चैतद्विद्मः कतरन्नो गरीयः
यद्वा जयेम यदि वा जयेयुः ।
यानेव हत्वा न जिजीविषामः
तेऽवस्थिताः प्रमुखे धार्तराष्ट्राः।।६।।

na caitadvidmaḥ kataranno garīyaḥ
yadvā jayema yadi vā no jayeyuḥ
yāneva hatvā na jijīviṣāmaḥ
te'vasthitāḥ pramukhe dhārtarāṣṭrāḥ (6)

कार्पण्यदोषोपहतस्वभावः
पृच्छामि त्वां धर्मसंमूढचेताः ।
यच्छ्रेयः स्यान्निश्चितं ब्रूहि तन्मे
शिष्यस्तेऽहं शाधि मां त्वां प्रपन्नम् ।। ७।।

kārpaṇyadoṣopahatasvabhāvaḥ
pṛcchāmi tvāṃ dharmasammūḍhacetāḥ
yacchreyaḥ syānniścitaṃ brūhi tanme
śiṣyaste'haṃ śādhi mām tvāṃ prapannam (7)

न हि प्रपश्यामि ममापनुद्याद्
यच्छोकमुच्छोषणमिन्द्रियाणाम् ।
अवाप्य भूमावसपत्नमृद्धं
राज्यं सुराणामपि चाधिपत्यम् ।।८।।

na hi prapaśyāmi mamāpanudyād
yacchokamucchoṣaṇamindriyāṇām
avāpya bhūmāvasapatnamṛddhaṃ
rājyaṃ surāṇāmapi cādhipatyam (8)

सञ्जय उवाच

एवमुक्त्वा हृषीकेशं गुडाकेशः परन्तपः ।
न योत्स्य इति गोविन्दमुक्त्वा तूष्णीं बभूव ह ॥ ९॥

तमुवाच हृषीकेशः प्रहसन्निव भारत ।
सेनयोरुभयोर्मध्ये विषीदन्तमिदं वचः ॥ १०॥

sañjaya uvāca

evamuktvā hṛṣīkeśaṃ guḍākeśaḥ parantapaḥ
na yotsya iti govindamuktvā tūṣṇīm babhūva ha (9)

tamuvāca hṛṣīkeśaḥ prahasanniva bhārata
senayorubhayormadhye viṣīdantamidaṃ vacaḥ (10)

श्री भगवान् उवाच

अशोच्यानन्वशोचस्त्वं प्रज्ञावादांश्च भाषसे ।
गतासूनगतासूंश्च नानुशोचन्ति पण्डिताः ॥ ११॥

śrī bhagavān uvāca
aśocyānanvaśocastvaṃ prajñāvādāṃśca bhāṣase
gatāsūnagatāsūṃśca nānuśocanti paṇḍitāḥ (11)

न त्वेवाहं जातु नाशं न त्वं नेमे जनाधिपाः।
न चैव न भविष्यामः सर्वे वयमतः परम् ॥ १२॥

na tvevahaṃ jātu nāśaṃ na tvaṃ neme janādhipāḥ
na caiva na bhaviṣyāmaḥ sarve vayamataḥ paraṃ (12)

देहिनोऽस्मिन्यथा देहे कौमारं यौवनं जरा।

तथा देहान्तरप्राप्तः धीरतत्र न मुह्यति ॥ १३॥

dehino'smin yathā dehe kaumāraṃ yauvanaṃ jarā
tathā dehāntaraprāptiḥ dhīrastatra na muhyati (13)

मात्रास्पर्शास्तु कौन्तेय शीतोष्णसुखदुःखदाः।
आगमापायिनोऽनित्याः तांस्तितिक्षस्व भारत ॥ १४॥

mātrāsparśāstu kaunteya śītoṣṇasukhaduḥkhadāḥ
āgamāpāyino'nityāḥ tāṃstitikṣasva bhārata (14)

यं हि न व्यथयन्त्येते पुरुषं पुरुषर्षभ।
समदुःखसुखं धीरं सोऽमृतत्वाय कल्पते ॥१५॥

yaṃ hi na vyathayantyete puruṣaṃ puruṣarṣabha
samaduḥkhasukhaṃ dhīraṃ so'mṛtatvāya kalpate (15)

नासतो विद्यते भावः नाभावो विद्यते सतः।
उभयोरपि दृष्टोऽन्तः त्वनयोस्तत्त्वदर्शिभिः ॥१६॥

nāsato vidyate bhāvaḥ nābhāvo vidyate sataḥ
ubhayorapi dṛṣṭo'ntaḥ tvanayostattvadarśibhiḥ (16)

अविनाशि तु तद्विद्धि येन सर्वमिदं ततम्।
विनाशमव्ययस्यास्य न कश्चित्कर्तुमर्हति ॥१७॥

avināśi tu tadviddhi yena sarvamidaṃ tatam
vināśamavyayasyāsya na kaścitkartumarhati (17)

अन्तवन्त इमे देहाः नित्यस्योक्ताः शरीरिणः।
अनाशिनोऽप्रमेयस्य तस्माद्युध्यस्व भारत ॥१८॥

antavanta ime dehāḥ nityasyoktāḥ śarīriṇaḥ
anāśino'prameyasya tasmādyudhyasva bhārata (18)

य एनं वेत्ति हन्तारं यश्चैनं मन्यते हतम् ।
उभौ तौ न विजानीतः नायं हन्ति न हन्यते ॥१९॥

ya enaṃ vetti hantāraṃ yaścainaṃ manyate hatam
ubhau tau na vijānītaḥ nāyaṃ hanti na hanyate (19)

न जायते म्रियते वा कदाचिद्
नायं भूत्वा भविता वा न भूयः।
अजो नित्यः शाश्वतोयं पुराणः
न हन्यते हन्यमाने शरीरे ॥२०॥

na jāyate mriyate vā kadācid
nāyaṃ bhūtvā bhavitā vā na bhūyaḥ
ajo nityaḥ śāśvato'yaṃ purāṇaḥ
na hanyate hanyamāne śarīre (20)

वेदाविनाशिनं नित्यं य एनमजमव्ययम् ।
कथं स पुरुषः पार्थ कं घातयति हन्ति कम् ॥ २१॥

vedāvināśinaṃ nityaṃ ya enamajamavyayam
kathaṃ sa puruṣaḥ pārtha kaṃ ghātayati hanti kam (21)

वासांसि जीर्णानि यथा विहाय
नवानि गृह्णाति नरोऽपराणि ।
तथा शरीराणि विहाय जीर्णानि
अन्यानि संयाति नवानि देही ॥ २२॥

vāsāṃsi jīrṇāni yathā vihāya
navāni gṛhṇāti naro'parāṇi
tathā śarīrāṇi vihāya jīrṇāni
anyāni saṃyāti navāni dehī (22)

नैनं छिन्दन्ति शस्त्राणि नैनं दहति पावकः।
न चैनं क्लेदयन्त्यापः न शोषयति मारुतः ॥ २३॥

nainaṃ chindanti śastrāṇi nainaṃ dahati pāvakaḥ
na cainaṃ kledayantyāpaḥ na śoṣayati mārutaḥ (23)

अच्छेद्योऽयमदाह्योयम् अक्लेद्योऽशोष्य एव च।
नित्यः सर्वगतः स्थाणुः अचलोऽयं सनातनः ॥ २४॥

acchedyo'yamadāhyo'yam akledyo'śoṣya eva ca
nityaḥ sarvagataḥ sthāṇuḥ acalo'yaṃ sanātanaḥ (24)

अव्यक्तोऽयमचिन्त्योऽयम् अविकार्योऽयमुच्यते।
तस्मादेवं विदित्वैनं नानुशोचितुमर्हसि ॥ २५॥

avyakto'yamacintyo'yam avikāryo'yamucyate
tasmādevaṃ viditvainaṃ nānuśocitumarhasi (25)

अथ चैनं नित्यजातं नित्यं वा मन्यसे मृतम्।
तथापि त्वं महाबाहो नैवं शोचितुमर्हसि ॥ २६॥

atha cainaṃ nityajātaṃ nityaṃ vā manyase mṛtam
tathāpi tvaṃ mahābāho naivaṃ śocitumarhasi (26)

जातस्य हि धृवो मृत्युः धृवं जन्म मृतस्य च।
तस्मादपरिहार्येऽर्थे न त्वं शोचितुमर्हसि ॥ २७॥

jātasya hi dhṛvo mṛtyuḥ dhṛuvaṃ janma mṛtasya ca
tasmādaparihārye'rthe na tvaṃ śocitumarhasi (27)

अव्यक्तादीनि भूतानि व्यक्तमध्यानि भारत।
अव्यक्तनिधनान्येव तत्र का परिदेवना ॥२८॥

avyaktādīni bhūtāni vyaktamadhyāni bhārata
avyaktanidhanānyeva tatra kā paridevanā (28)

आश्चर्यवत्पश्यति कश्चिदेनम्
आश्चर्यवद्वदति तथैव चान्यः।
आश्चर्यवच्चैनमन्यः श्रृणोति
श्रुत्वाप्येनं वेद न चैव कश्चित्॥२९॥

āścaryavatpaśyati kaścidenam
āścaryavadvadati tathaiva cānyaḥ
āścaryavaccainamanyaḥ śṛṇoti
śrutvāpyenaṃ veda na caiva kaścit (29)

देही नित्यमवध्योऽयं देहे सर्वस्य भारत।
तस्मात्सर्वाणि भूतानि न त्वं शोचितुमर्हसि॥ ३०॥

dehī nityamavadhyo'yaṃ dehe sarvasya bhārata
tasmātsarvāṇi bhūtāni na tvaṃ śocitumarhasi (30)

स्वधर्ममपि चावेक्ष्य न विकम्पितुमर्हसि।
धर्म्याद्धियुद्धाच्छ्रेयोऽन्यत् क्षत्रियस्य न विद्यते ॥३१॥

svadharmamapi cāvekṣya na vikampitumarhasi
dharmyāddhiyudhācchreyo'nyat kṣatriyasya na vidyate (31)

यदृच्छया चोपपन्नं स्वर्गद्वारमपावृतम्।
सुखिनः क्षत्रियाः पार्थ लभन्ते युध्दमीदृशम् ॥ ३२॥

yadṛcchayā copapannaṃ svargadvāramapāvṛtam
sukhinaḥ kṣatriyāḥ pārtha labhante yuddhamīdṛśam (32)

अथ चेत्त्वमिमं धर्म्यं सङ्ग्रामं न करिष्यसि ।
ततः स्वधर्मं कीर्तिं च हित्वा पापमवाप्स्यसि ।।३३।।

atha cettvamimaṃ dhramyaṃ saṅgrāmaṃ na kariṣyasi
tataḥ svadharmaṃ kīrtiṃ ca hitvā pāpamavāpsyasi (33)

अकीर्तिञ्चापि भूतानि कथयिष्यन्ति तेऽव्ययाम् ।
सम्भावितस्य चाकीर्तिः मरणादपिरिच्यते ।।३४।।

akīrtiñcāpi bhūtāni kathayiṣyanti te'vyayām
sambhāvitasya cākīrtiḥ maraṇādatiricyate (34)

भयाद्रणादुपरतं मंस्यन्ते त्वां महारथाः ।
येषां च त्वं बहुमतः भूत्वा यास्यसि लाघवम् ।। ३५।।

bhayādraṇāduparataṃ maṃsyante tvāṃ mahārathāḥ
yeṣāṃ tvaṃ ca bahumataḥ bhūtvā yāsyasi lāghavam (35)

अवाच्यवादांश्च बहून् वदिष्यन्ति तवाहिताः ।
निन्दन्तस्तव सामर्थ्यं ततो दुःखतरं नु किम् ।।३६।।

avācyavādāṃśca bahūn vadiṣyanti tavāhitāḥ
nindantastava sāmarthyaṃ tato duḥkhataraṃ nu kim (36)

हतो वा प्राप्स्यसि स्वर्गं जित्वा वा भोक्ष्यसे महीम्।
तस्मादुत्तिष्ठ कौन्तेय युद्धाय कृतनिश्चयः।।३७।।

hato vā prāpsyasi svargaṃ jitvā vā bhokṣyase mahīm
tasmāduttiṣṭha kaunteya yuddhāya kṛtaniścayaḥ (37)

सुखदुःखे समे कृत्वा लाभालाभौ जयाजयौ ।
ततो युद्धाय युज्यस्व नैवं पापमवाप्स्यसि ।।३८।।

sukhaduḥke same kṛtvā lābhālābhau jayājayau
tato yuddhāya yujyasva naivaṃ pāpamavāpsyasi (38)

एषा तेऽभिहिता साङ्ख्ये बुद्धिर्योगे त्विमां शृणु ।
बुद्ध्या युक्तो यया पार्थ कर्मबन्धं प्रहास्यसि।। ३९।।

eṣā te'bhihitā sāṅkhye bhddhiryoge tvimām śṛṇu
bhddhyā yukto yayā pārtha karmabandhaṃ prahāsyasi (39)

नेहाभिक्रमनाशोऽस्ति प्रत्यवायो न विद्यते ।
स्वल्पमप्यस्य धर्मस्य त्रायते महतो भयात् ॥४०॥

nehābhikramanāśo'sti pratyavāyo na vidyate
svalpamapyasya dharmasya trāyate mahato bhayāt (40)

व्यवसायात्मिका बुद्धिः एकेह कुरुनन्दन ।
बहुशाखा ह्यनन्ताश्च बुद्धयोऽव्यवसायिनाम् ॥४१॥

vyavasāyātmikā buddhiḥ ekeha kurunandana
bahuśākhā hyanantāśca buddhayo'vyavasāyinām (41)

यामिमां पुष्पितां वाचं प्रवदन्त्यविपश्चितः।
वेदवादरताः पार्थ नान्यदस्तीति वादिनः ॥४२॥

yāmimāṃ puṣpitāṃ vācaṃ pravadantyavipaścitaḥ
vedavādaratāḥ pārtha nanyadastīti vādinaḥ (42)

कामात्मानः स्वर्गपराः जन्मकर्मफलप्रदाम् ।
क्रियाविशेषबहुलां भोगैश्वर्यगतिं प्रति ॥४३॥

kāmātmānaḥ svargaparāḥ janmakarma phalapradām
kriyāviśeṣabahulāṃ bhogaiśvaryagatiṃ prati (43)

भोगैश्वर्यप्रसक्तानां तयापहृतचेतसाम् ।
व्यवसायात्मिका बुद्धिः समाधौ न विधीयते ॥४४ ॥

bhogaiśvaryaprasaktānāṃ tayāpahṛtacetasām
vyavasāyātmikā buddhiḥ samādhau na vidhīyate (44)

त्रैगुण्यविषया वेदाः निस्त्रैगुण्यो भवार्जुन ।
निर्द्वन्द्वो नित्यसत्त्वस्थः निर्योगक्षेम आत्मवान् ॥४५॥

traiguṇyaviṣayā vedāḥ nistraiguṇyo bhavārjuna
nirdvandvo nityasattvasthaḥ niryogakṣema ātmavān (45)

यावानर्थ उदपाने सर्वतस्सम्प्लुतोदके ।
तावान्सर्वेषु वेदेषु ब्राह्मणस्य विजानतः॥४६॥

yāvānartha udapāne sarvatassamplutodake
tāvān sarveṣu vedeṣu brāhmaṇasya vijānataḥ (46)

कर्मण्येवाधिकारस्ते मा फलेषु कदाचन ।
माकर्मफलहेतुर्भूः मा ते सङ्गोऽस्त्वकर्मणि ॥४७॥

karmaṇyevādhikāraste mā phaleṣu kadācana
mā karmaphalaheturbhūḥ mā te saṅgo'stvakarmaṇi (47)

योगस्थः कुरु कर्माणि सङ्गं त्यक्त्वा धनञ्जय ।
सिद्ध्यसिद्ध्योः समो भूत्वा समत्वं योग उच्यते ॥४८॥

yogasthaḥ kuru karmāṇi saṅgaṃ tyaktvā dhanañjaya
siddhyasiddhyoḥ samo bhūtvā samatvaṃ yoga ucyate (48)

दूरेण ह्यवरं कर्म बुद्धियोगाद्धनञ्जय।
बुद्धौ शरणमन्विच्छ कृपणाः फलहेतवः॥४९॥

dūreṇa hyavaraṃ karma buddhiyogāddhanañjaya
buddhau śaraṇamanviccha kṛpaṇāḥ phalahetavaḥ (49)

बुद्धियुक्तो जहातीह उभे सुकृतदुष्कृते ।
तस्माद्योगाय युज्यस्व योगः कर्मसु कौशलम् ॥५०॥

bhuddhiyukto jahātīha ubhe sukṛtaduṣkṛte
tasmādyogāya yujyasva yogaḥ karmasu kauśalam (50)

कर्मजं बुद्धियुक्ता हि फलं त्यक्त्वा मनीषिणः ।
जन्मबन्धविनिर्मुक्ताः पदं गच्छन्त्यनामयम् ॥ ५२॥

karmajaṃ bhddhiyuktā hi phalaṃ tyaktvā manīṣiṇaḥ
janmabandhavinirmuktāḥ padaṃ gacchantyanāmayam (51)

यदा ते मोहकलिलं बुद्धिर्व्यतितरिष्यति ।
तदा गन्तासि निर्वेदं श्रोतव्यस्य श्रुतस्य च ॥५२॥

yadā te mohakalilaṃ buddhirvyatitariṣyati
tadā gantāsi nirvedaṃ śrotavyasya śrutasya ca (52)

श्रुतिविप्रतिपन्ना ते यदा स्थास्यति निश्चला।
समाधावचला बुद्धिः तदा योगमवाप्स्यसि ॥५३॥

śrutivipratipanna te yadā sthāsyati niścalā
samādhāvacalā buddhiḥ tadā yogamavāpsyasi (53)

अर्जुन उवाच

स्थितप्रज्ञस्य का भाषा समाधिस्थस्य केशव ।
स्थितधीः किं प्रभाषेत किमासीत व्रजेत किम् ॥५४॥

arjuna uvāca

sthitaprajñasya kā bhāṣā samādhisthasya keśava
sthitadhīḥ kiṃ prabhāṣeta kimāsīta vrajeta kim (54)

श्री भगवान् उवाच
प्रजहाति यदा कामान्सर्वान्पार्थ मनोगतान् ।
आत्मन्येवात्मना तुष्टः स्थितप्रज्ञस्तदोच्यते ॥ ५५॥

śrī bhagavān uvāca
prajahāti yadā kāmān sarvānpārtha manogatān
ātmanyevātmanā tuṣṭaḥ sthitaprajñastadocyate (55)

दुःखेष्वनुद्विग्नमनाः सुखेषु विगतस्पृहः।
वीतरागभयक्रोधः स्थितधीर्मुनिरुच्यते ॥ ५६॥

duḥkheṣvanudvignamanāḥ sukheṣu vigataspṛhaḥ
vītarāgabhayakrodhaḥ sthitadhīrmunirucyate (56)

यः सर्वत्रानभिस्नेहः तत्तत्प्राप्य शुभाशुभम् ।
नाभिनन्दति न द्वेष्टि तस्य प्रज्ञा प्रतिष्ठिता ॥ ५७ ॥

yaḥ sarvatrānabhisnehaḥ tattatprāpya śubhāśubham
nābhinandati na dveṣṭi tasya prajñā pratiṣṭhitā (57)

यदासंहरते चायं कूर्मोऽङ्गानीव सर्वशः ।
इन्द्रियाणीन्द्रियार्थेभ्यः तस्य प्रज्ञा प्रतिष्ठिता ॥५८॥

yadā saṃharate cāyaṃ kūrmo'ṅgānīva sarvaśaḥ
indriyāṇīndriyārthebhyaḥ tasya prajñā pratiṣṭhitā (58)

विषया विनिवर्तन्ते निराहारस्य देहिनः।
रसवर्जं रसोऽप्यस्य परं दृष्ट्वा निवर्तते ॥५९॥

viṣayā vinivartante nirāhārasya dehinaḥ
rasavarjam raso'pyasya paraṃ dṛṣṭvā nivartate (59)

यततो ह्यपि कौन्तेय पुरुषस्य विपश्चितः ।
इन्द्रियाणि प्रमाथीनि हरन्ति प्रसभं मनः ॥ ६० ॥

yatato hyapi kaunteya puruṣasya vipaścitaḥ
indriyāṇi pramāthīni haranti prasabhaṃ manaḥ (60)

तानि सर्वाणि संयम्य युक्त आसीत मत्परः ।
वशे हि यस्येन्द्रियाणि तस्य प्रज्ञा प्रतिष्ठिता ॥ ६१ ॥

tāni sarvāṇi saṃyamya yukta āsīta matparaḥ
vaśe hi yasyendriyāṇi tasya prajñā pratiṣṭhitā (61)

ध्यायतो विषयान् पुंसः सङ्गस्तेषूपजायते ।
सङ्गात्सञ्जायते कामः कामात्क्रोधोऽभिजायते ॥ ६२ ॥

क्रोधाद्भवति सम्मोहः सम्मोहात्स्मृतिविभ्रमः ।
स्मृतिभ्रंशाद् बुद्धिनाशः बुद्धिनाशात्प्रणश्यति ॥ ६३ ॥

dhyāyato viṣayān puṃsaḥ saṅgasteṣūpajāyate
saṅgātsañjāyate kāmaḥ kāmātkrodho'bhijāyate (62)

krodhādbhavati sammohaḥ sammohātsmṛtivibhramaḥ
smṛtibhraṃśād buddhināśaḥ buddhināśātpraṇaśyati (63)

रागद्वेषवियुक्तैस्तु विषयानिन्द्रियैश्चरन् ।
आत्मवश्यैर्विधेयात्मा प्रसादमधिगच्छति ॥ ६४ ॥

rāgadveṣaviyuktaistu viṣayānindriyaiścaran
ātmavaśyairvidheyātmā prasādamadhigacchati (64)

प्रसादे सर्वदुःखानां हानिरस्योपजायते ।
प्रसन्न चेतसो ह्याशु बुद्धिः पर्यवतिष्ठते ॥ ६५ ॥

prasāde sarvaduḥkhānāṃ hānirasyopajāyate
prasannacetaso hyāśu buddhiḥ paryavatiṣṭhate (65)

नास्ति बुद्धिरयुक्तस्य न चायुक्तस्य भावना ।
न चाभावयतः शान्तिः अशान्तस्य कुतः सुखम् ॥ ६६ ॥

nāsti buddhirayuktasya na cāyuktasya bhāvanā
na cābhāvayataḥ śāntiḥ aśāntasya kutaḥ sukham (66)

इन्द्रियाणां हि चरतां यन्मनोऽनुविधीयते।
तदस्य हरति प्रज्ञां वायुर्नावमिवाम्भसि ॥६७॥

indriyāṇāṃ hi caratāṃ yanmano'nuvidhīyate
tadasya harati prajñāṃ vāyurnāvamivāmbhasi (67)

तस्माद्यस्य महाबाहो निगृहीतानि सर्वशः ।
इन्द्रियाणीन्द्रियार्थेभ्यः तस्य प्रज्ञा प्रतिष्ठिता ॥६८॥

tasmādyasya mahābāho nigṛhītāni sarvaśaḥ
indriyāṇīndriyārthebhyaḥ tasya prajñā pratiṣṭhitā (68)

या निशा सर्वभूतानां तस्यां जागर्ति संयमी।
यस्यां जाग्रति भूतानि सा निशा पश्यतो मुनेः ॥६९॥

yā niśā sarvabhūtānāṃ tasyāṃ jāgarti saṃyamī
yasyāṃ jāgrati bhūtāni sā niśā paśyato muneḥ (69)

आपूर्यमाणमचलप्रतिष्ठं
समुद्रमापः प्रविशन्ति यद्वत् ।
तद्वत्कामा यं प्रविशन्ति सर्वे
स शान्तिमाप्नोति न कामकामी ॥७०॥

āpūryamāṇamacalapratiṣṭham
samudramapaḥ praviśanti yadvat
tadvatkāmā yaṃ praviśanti sarve
sa śāntimāpnoti na kāmakāmī (70)

विहाय कामान्यस्सर्वान्पुमांश्चरति निस्पृहः।
निर्ममो निरहङ्कारः स शान्तिमधिगच्छति ॥७१॥

vihāya kāmānyassarvānpumāṃścarati nissprhaḥ
nirmamo nirahaṅkārah sa śāntimadhigacchati (71)

एषा ब्राह्मी स्थितिः पार्थ नैनां प्राप्य विमुह्यति ।
स्थित्वास्यामन्तकालेऽपि ब्रह्मनिर्वाणमृच्छति ॥७२॥

eṣā brāhmī sthitiḥ pārtha naināṃ prāpya vimuhyati
sthitvāsyāmantakāle'pi brahmanirvāṇamṛcchati (72)

ॐ तत् सत् इति श्रीमद्भगवद्गीतासु उपनिषत्सु ब्रह्मविद्यायां योगशास्त्रे श्रीकृष्णार्जुनसंवादे साङ्ख्ययोगो नाम द्वितीयोध्यायः ॥

oṃ tat sat iti śrīmadbhagavadgītāsu upaniṣatsu brahmavidyāyāṃ yogaśāstre śrīkṛṣṇārjunasaṃvāde sāṅkhyayogo nāma dvitīyodhyāyaḥ

Nirvāṇaṣaṭkam

मनोबुद्ध्यहङ्कारचित्तानि नाहं þ
न च श्रोत्रजिह्वे न च घ्राणनेत्रे ।
न च व्योम भूमिर्न तेजो न वायुः
चिदानन्दरूपश्शिवोऽहं शिवोऽहम् ॥१॥ (चिदा...)

manobhuddhyahankāracittāni nāhaṃ
na ca śrotrajihve na ca ghrāṇanetre
na ca vyoma bhūmirna tejo na vāyuḥ
cidānandarūpaśśivo'haṃ śivo'ham (1) (*cidā...*)

manobhuddhyahankāracittāni - the mind, the intellect, the ego and the memory; *na* - not; *āhaṃ* - I am; *na* - not; *ca* - and; *śrotrajihve* - the ear-the tongue; *na* - not; *ca* - and; *ghrāṇanetre* - the nose and the eyes; *na* - not; *ca* - and; *vyoma* - the space; *bhūmir* - the earth; *na* - not; *tejaḥ* - the fire; *na* - not; *vāyuḥ* - the wind; *cidānandarūpaḥ* - the nature of consciousness and limitless; *śivaḥ* - pure self; *aham* - I am; *śivaḥ* - pure self; *aham* - I am

I am not the mind, intellect, memory nor ego. Nor am I the ears nor tongue. I am not the nose nor eyes, nor the space, earth, fire or wind. I am of the nature of consciousness and limitlessness. I am pure self.

न च प्राणसंज्ञो न वै पञ्चवायुः
न वा सप्तधातुर्न वा पञ्चकोशाः।
न वाक् पाणिपादौ न चोपस्थवायुः
चिदानन्दरूपश्शिवोऽहं शिवोऽहम् ॥ २॥ (चिदा...)

na ca prāṇasaṃjño na vai pañcavāyuḥ
na vā saptadhāturna vā pañcakośāḥ
na vāk pāṇipādau na copasthapāyuḥ
cidānandarūpaśśivo'haṃ śivo'ham (2) (*cidā...*)

na - not; *ca* - and; *prāṇasaṃjñaḥ* - the *na* - not; *vai* - indeed; *pañcavāyuḥ* - the five *prāṇas*; *na* - not; *vā* - or; *saptadhātuḥ* - the seven constituents of the body; *na* - not; *vā* - or; *pañcakośāḥ* - the five sheaths; *na* - not; *vāk* - the organ of speech; *pāṇipādau* - hands and legs; *na* - not; *ca* - and; *upasthapāyū* - the genital and the anus; *cidānandarūpaḥ* - the nature of consciousness and limitless; *śivaḥ* - pure self; *aham* - I am; *śivaḥ* - pure self; *aham* - I am

I am not the life breath nor am I the five *prāṇas*. I am not the seven constituents of the body, nor am I the five sheaths. I am not the organ of speech nor hands and legs. Nor am I the genital nor anus. I am of the nature of consciousness and limitlessness. I am pure self.

न मे द्वेषरागौ न मे लोभमोहौ
मदौ नैव मे नैव मात्सर्यभावः ।
न धर्मो न चार्थो न कामो न मोक्षः
चिदानन्दरूपश्शिवोऽहं शिवोऽहम् ॥३॥ (चिदा...)

na me dveṣarāgau na me lobhamohau
mado naiva me naiva mātsaryabhāvaḥ
na dharmo na cārtho na kāmo na mokṣaḥ
cidānandarūpaśśivo'haṃ śivo'ham (3) (*cidā*...)

na - not; *me* - for me; *dveṣarāgau* - likes and dislikes; *na* - not; *me* - for me; *lobhamohau* - greed and delusion; *madaḥ* - pride; *na* - do not have; *eva* - at all; *mātsaryabhāvaḥ* - jealousy; *na* - not; *dharmaḥ* - the pursuit of *dharma*; *na* - not; *ca* - and; *arthaḥ* - the pursuit of security; *na* - not; *kāmaḥ* - the pursuit of pleasures; *na* - not; *mokṣaḥ* - the pursuit of freedom; *cidānandarūpaḥ* - the nature of consciousness and limitless; *śivaḥ* - pure self; *aham* - I am; *śivaḥ* - pure self; *aham* - I am

I do not have likes, dislikes, greed and delusion. I do not have pride. Nor do I have jealousy. I do not have pursuit of *dharma*, security, pleasures or freedom. I am of the nature of consciousness and limitlessness. I am pure self.

न पुण्यं न पापं न सौख्यं न दुःखं
न मन्त्रो न तीर्थं न वेदा न यज्ञाः।
अहं भोजनं नैव भोज्यं न भोक्ता
चिदानन्दरूपश्शिवोऽहं शिवोऽहम् ॥४॥ (चिदा...)

na puṇyaṃ na pāpaṃ na saukhyaṃ na duḥkhaṃ
na mantro na tīrthaṃ na vedā na yajñāḥ
ahaṃ bhojanaṃ naiva bhojyaṃ na bhoktā
cidānandarūpaśśivo'haṃ śivo'ham (4) (*cidā*...)

na - not; *puṇyam* - *puṇya*; *na* - not; *pāpam* - *pāpa*; *na* - not; *saukhyam* - happiness; *na* - not; *duḥkham* - sorrow; *na* - not; *mantraḥ* - *mantra*; *na* - not; *tīrtham* - holy place; *na* - not; *vedāḥ* - *Vedas*; *na* - not; *yajñāḥ* - fire rituals; *aham* - I am; *bhojanam* - the action of experience; *na* - not; *eva* - at all; *bhojyam* - the object of experience; *na* - not; *bhoktā* - the experiencer; *cidānandarūpaḥ* - the nature of consciousness and limitless; *śivaḥ* - pure self; *aham* - I am; *śivaḥ* - pure self; *aham* - I am

There is no *puṇya* or *pāpa* or happiness or sorrow for me. Nor *mantra*, holy place, *Vedas* or fire rituals exist (for me), I am neither an experience nor the object of experience nor the experiencer. I am of the nature of consciousness and limitlessness. I am pure self.

न मे मृत्युशङ्का न मे जातिभेदः
पिता नैव मे नैव माता न जन्म।
न बन्धुर्न मित्रं गुरुर्नैव शिष्यः
चिदानन्दरूपश्शिवोऽहं शिवोऽहम् ॥५॥ (चिदा...)

na me mṛtyuśaṅkhā na me jātibhedaḥ
pitā naiva me naiva mātā na janma
na bandhurna mitraṃ gururnaiva śiśyaḥ
cidānandarūpaśśivo'haṃ śivo'ham (5) (*cidā...*)

na - not; *me* - for me; *mṛtyuśaṅkhā* - doubts about death; *na* - not; *me* - for me; *jātibhedaḥ* - caste differences; *pitā* - father; *na* - not; *eva* - at all; *mātā* - mother; *na* - not; *janma* - birth; *na* - not; *bandhuḥ* - relative; *na* - not; *mitram* - friend; *guruḥ* - teacher; *na* - not; *eva* - at all; *śiśyaḥ* - student; *cidānandarūpaḥ* - the nature of consciousness and limitless; *śivaḥ* - pure self; *aham* - I am; *śivaḥ* - pure self; *aham* - I am

There is no death or doubts or caste differences in me. There is no father, mother, or birth for me. There is no relative or friend or teacher or student (for me). I am of the nature of consciousness and limitlessness. I am pure self.

अहं निर्विकल्पो निराकाररूपः
विभुत्वाच्च सर्वत्र सर्वेन्द्रियाणाम्।
न चासाङ्गतो नैव मुक्तिर्न बन्धः
चिदानन्दरूपश्शिवोऽहं शिवोऽहम् ॥६॥ (चिदा...)

ahaṃ nirvikalpo nirākārarūpaḥ
vibhutvācca sarvatra sarvendriyāṇām
na cāsaṅgato naivamuktirna bandhaḥ
cidānandarūpaśśivo'haṃ śivo'ham (6) (*cidā...*)

aham - I am; *nirvikalpaḥ* - free of thoughts; *nirākārarūpaḥ* - free of forms; *vibhutvāt* - being pervasive; *ca* - and; *sarvatra* - everywhere; *sarvendriyāṇām* - of all sence organs; *na* - not; *ca* - and; *asaṅgato* - unconnected; *na* - not; *eva* - at all; *muktiḥ* - freedom; *na* - not; *bandhaḥ* - bondage; *cidānandarūpaḥ* - the nature of consciousness and limitless; *śivaḥ* - pure self; *aham* - I am; *śivaḥ* - pure self; *aham* - I am

I am free of thoughts, and free of forms. I am connected to all sense organs as I pervade everywhere. There is no freedom of bondage in me. I am of the nature of consciousness and limitlessness. I am pure self.

Made in the USA
Middletown, DE
01 October 2023

39916571R00086